TECH SMART

The Perfect Storm

JOHN R. CONNELLY

Copyright © 2019 John R. Connelly.

All rights reserved. No part of this book may be used or reproduced by any means, graphic, electronic, or mechanical, including photocopying, recording, taping or by any information storage retrieval system without the written permission of the author except in the case of brief quotations embodied in critical articles and reviews.

The information, ideas, and suggestions in this book are not intended to render professional advice. Before following any suggestions contained in this book, you should consult your personal accountant or other financial advisor. Neither the author nor the publisher shall be liable or responsible for any loss or damage allegedly arising as a consequence of your use or application of any information or suggestions in this book.

Archway Publishing books may be ordered through booksellers or by contacting:

Archway Publishing
1663 Liberty Drive
Bloomington, IN 47403
www.archwaypublishing.com
1 (888) 242-5904

Because of the dynamic nature of the Internet, any web addresses or links contained in this book may have changed since publication and may no longer be valid. The views expressed in this work are solely those of the author and do not necessarily reflect the views of the publisher, and the publisher hereby disclaims any responsibility for them.

Any people depicted in stock imagery provided by Getty Images are models, and such images are being used for illustrative purposes only. Certain stock imagery © Getty Images.

ISBN: 978-1-4808-8534-9 (sc)
ISBN: 978-1-4808-8536-3 (hc)
ISBN: 978-1-4808-8535-6 (e)

Library of Congress Control Number: 2019919530

Print information available on the last page.

Archway Publishing rev. date: 12/27/2019

Contents

The Dedication vii
Overview... ix
Keys to succeed xi
Acknowledgment xiii
'The Perfect Storm System... xv
Accumulation/Distribution 1
Arms Index 5
Average Directional Movement 9
Bollinger Bands... 13
Bulls Vs. Bears.. 17
Chaiken Money Flow... 19
The Commodity Channel Index 23
Call/Put Volume & Open Interest 27
Fibonacci... 31
52 Week High 52 Week Low Formula 35
Moving Average Convergence/Divergence............................... 39
Money Flow 43
Moving Averages 47
Open 10 TRIN Trading Index 51
Parabolic SAR 57
Pivot Point with Fibonacci Points 61
Price Momentum 65
Pring's Know Sure Thing.. 69
Rate of Change 73
Relative Strength Index 77

Stochastic Oscillator	81
Trend	85
True Strength Index	89
Volatility	91
Volume	93
Pivot Points	95
Fibonacci	99
Stock Check List	105
What are options?	109
How to tell if an Option is IN, AT or OUT of the Money	119
Input Data Sheet	123
Summary Sheet	131
S&P Formula Spreadsheet	133
Overall Market Spreadsheet	145
World Markets	159
How to Pick Top Stocks	161
How to Analyze A Stock	167
Stock check up	177
Perfect Storm Tracking Results	183
Details of Selections	185
Portfolio Performance	189
Work Cited	193
Legal Disclaimer	197

The Dedication

To the people that dream for something better,
for their families and for themselves.
This system could help you get closer to that dream.

You are responsible for your life
discovery is a process
Everything in life is a journey
An obstacle is a way forward
Knowing yourself leads to wisdom
Good luck to all that dare

Overview

To make the perfect storm work it is going to take a few key components, first is dedication and discipline, every day we must get the numbers and input them correctly into our system, it will only take around, an hour a day but it must be done every day with out fail. The second most important thing is to analyze the data that is being generated daily and look for the primary trend. The third and one of the most important thing is, do not get greedy, do not fall in love with a stock or sector, keep to you plan and sell or take profits when you hit your designated percentages and cut a stock or sector when it declines never double down on a stock when it is declining. Always be on the same side as the primary trend.

Tech smart will help you pick stocks that have the best chance of making money, why not have a portfolio with all, all-stars in it, all stars that are being accumulated, that is a key factor as you will see. Tech smart will also provide information on how to analyze your picks and help choose the best stock to invest in. we will also provide useful information, that will check you picks by using over thirty different indicators that will provide a rating system for your stock.

There are several things that are key to mastering this system, first always be looking for the perfect storm. When all the indicators are in line 100% bullish or 100% bearish that is the perfect storm the market should change in direction and this is a key indicator. the second most important thing is always being on the same side as the primary trend, this will improve your chances of winning by seventy percent. The third most important thing is never use one formula or indicator to pick a stock or to buy or sell an issue.

The last and key factor to making this system work is gathering all the data and information we need to generate our formula's. the investor business daily is where we get most of our data from. They have an online weekly paper that generates so much useful data. We also get the stock checkup information from the research section of the investment business daily. The other format that will be needed is the wall street journal, this is free online, the two sections we use for most of our data is the markets data and the international markets, specifically the international stock indexes. The best free web site we like to use is stock charts .com, this is a great site that is easy to view multiple formulas at the same time. The site provides overlays and indicators, that can be viewed at a glance, and has the capacity to format, three overlays and indicators at the same time. There is one book that is a must, technical analysis A to Z by Steven Achelis, this book will review all the formulas, that are used by traders and investor, and will give you a helpful understanding of the formula's.

Keys to succeed

Dream big while setting realistic goals
Create a game plan to accomplish the goals
Install a system to complete the game plan
Provide clear and precise direction for the system
Think simplicity do not over complicate the issues
Focus on the big picture analyzing the day to day
Understand the numbers build analytic platforms
Be accessible and build relationships
Stay focused and tune out the distractions
Buckle down work smart and be disciplined
Compensate for your short comings with others
Learn from your mistakes and be persistent
Balance the fine line between ego and humility

Acknowledgment

All the long hours studying and inputting, all the different formulas by hand, the endless stacks of papers and spreadsheets reviewed with out the use of a computer. I feel it gave us a greater knowledge and understanding and respect, for the formulas we work with daily. I would like to thank my parents for all the information and data they generated, so I could pursue my vision. I would like to thank Omar Bennett for all his help gather all the information daily, and his vast knowledge of the markets and formulas. I would like to thank Gary griffin for his input on the markets, stock and options. I will not forget all our long discussions on the trends and position of the market and stocks. The man that made it possible and my mentor is Richard stock, all the long days studying the technical analysts A to Z, I would not have been able to get through it without your help. The general knowledge of the markets and option he possesses, and the way he can explain a vastly complicated subject in layman's term is truly a great talent. I owe him a debt I can only try to repay thank you my friend. I would like to thank my children for putting up with my long hours staring at the computer looking for the trend or the next profitable pick. The last and most important person is my partner in everything, my beautiful woman, that puts up with the daily grid of gathering, inputting, tracking, and analyzing the data, thank you Cathy Danzo. Having you by my side, I am able to concentrate on the task at hand and lose myself in the numbers with out feeling guilty thank you for being so selfless and kind.

'The Perfect Storm System

The Perfect Storm System consists of several formulas working together to determine the trend (Bullish or Bearish) of an index or security. We have developed several triggers using the Perfect Storm System that will signal a confirmed change in direction as well. Understanding the Perfect Storm System and these triggers will help an investor take greater advantage of price momentum, or limit their exposure when momentum is moving against them.

Knowing the direction of the market is key, for any trader, and can be valuable as well for an active investor. There are many vehicles for traders to make profits in Bullish and Bearish Markets (options, short selling, etc.). For long-term investors, knowing the trends can also be helpful, if they actively move into cash positions in down trends and stay fully invested in uptrends. Therefore, the Perfect Storm System can be invaluable in helping traders and investors to determine the current trend, and when that trend is changing.

We have found that trading the same direction as the market will increase your chances of a profitable trade. Predicting the absolute bottom or top for an index or security regularly is extremely difficult. To increase your chances of being correct, when the index or security look to be changing direction, wait for the change to occur and get confirmation of the change. Generally, by doing so, you can still capture 70-80% of the move, but you have increased your chances of being in a positive trade significantly. The Perfect Storm System will provide you with a confirmed turning point.

The Perfect Storm System uses over 20 technical and fundamental indicators determine the direction of the overall market. Some of the indicators we use are:

- Arms Index
- Volatility Index (VIX)
- Bull vs. Bear Ratio
- Open Interest – Call and Put Options
- Relative Strength Index
- Price Momentum
- Call vs. Put Premium Ratio
- Open 10 TRIN
- High Low Index
- Stochastic (slow and fast)
- Moving Averages (various time frames)
- Moving Average Convergence/Divergence (MACD)
- Accumulation Distribution Trend
- Chaikin Money Flow
- Commodity Channel Index
- Parabolic SAR
- Bollinger Bands
- Prings Know Sure Thing
- Average Directional Movement
- True Strength
- Fibonacci Retracements
- Pivot Points

The option information provides important insight into the psychology of market traders. The Premium Ratio can tell an investor where option traders think there is more risk to the market (Bullish or Bearish). All things considered, when Put Premiums are higher than Call Premiums, traders see more downside risk (Bearish) to the market. This signal is more of a preliminary signal, meaning it will usually start turning before pricing does. Again, you do not want to try and pick the turning point for an index or security, but when you start to see this indicator turn, you do want to start paying attention to your positions and evaluate the continued strength of the trend you are in. If you are in an uptrend, and you have been trading to take advantage of that, when this signal turns, it may be time to take profits and move into cash.

The Perfect Storm System considers all the indicators together and provides a confirmation of trend when 67% of indicators are aligned in one direction. There are three trends in the movement of an index or security: a primary, secondary and a minor trend. We will discuss these in more detail later in the book, but for the most part, we want to focus on the primary trend, as this is usually the strongest trend and outperforms the secondary and tertiary trends in most cases. The Perfect Storm System uses shorter and longer time periods for various indicators to determine the primary trend and reduce the chances for an inaccurate prediction. Because of this, there may be fewer signals, and more time before a change in direction signal is given. But when it is given, it is a stronger signal with a greater likelihood of being correct.

When using the Perfect Storm System to analyze a security, it is best to use this in conjunction with the overall indexes. It is possible that for an individual security, the trend may be Bullish and the indexes may be Bearish. In this instance, it is best to wait for the indexes to turn Bullish before entering any trades. Otherwise, the individual security may end up turning Bearish if the overall markets stay Bearish. Trading with the markets will increase your chances for a profitable trade.

The Perfect Storm System cannot pick or choose the security or index that you should trade. But, once you have selected an index or security, the Perfect Storm System will tell you the primary trend that security or index is in. And, if you continue using the Perfect Storm System, you will get a trigger/confirmation for when that trend has changed.

However, when looking for in individual security to trade, the first thing we look for is a sector leader. Sector leaders are the All-Stars, and are the stocks that outperform the S&P 500, and other securities in their sector. IBD ranks the performance of 33 sectors, and tracks the sector's rank over time so that you can see whether the sector is getting stronger or weaker. Typically, we select stocks that are in the top 5 sectors. We also look to the Investor's Business Daily (IBD) Top 50. This is a great source for securities that are outperforming all other securities and have strong fundamentals. The next area to look for securities is in the World Markets. IBD provides a list of the Top 10 World Stocks. All these tools will lead you to the top performing stocks, especially when markets are in an uptrend. Taking advantage of these trends will allow you to maximize profits. And then, when trends start to change, you can minimize losses. Together, this strategy will help you to yield results better than the indexes themselves, or even most mutual funds.

Now that we know where to find our top-rated stocks, we need to go to work and evaluate the securities/indexes we have selected. The goal is to determine whether their primary trend is up (Bullish) or down (Bearish). We need to put our securities to the test. IBD provides a stock checkup section that will give you great information on the strength of your stock. The first thing to look at is the IBD Composite Rating, you want to a composite rating of 90 (Percentile Raking out of 100). Second, we look at the Earnings Per Share (EPS) growth rating. Here, you want to see a top 5 rating and an EPS of 90. The third thing to look for is the relative strength rating. You want to see a top 5 rating and a RSI of 90. Next, you want to look at the IBD Sales and Profit Margin and Rate of Return (SMR). Again you want to see a top 5 rating and a SMR of A or B (The scale ranges from A – the best performing to E – the worst performing). For Rate of Return (ROE), you should look for a minimum 17% annually.

Once you have determined that a security has met the above we criteria, you want to check the security's Accumulation Distribution Rating in IBD. This rating uses IBD's proprietary method for analyzing stock price movements and associated volume, and then scores the security from A to E. An A rating means the stock is being accumulated by institutional investors and has increased volume on days the stock price was up, and on days when the stock price is lower, it is on lower volume. An E rating means that the stock is under distribution and is being sold by institutional investors. This would be evidenced by higher volume on days when the stock price is lower. This rating also evaluates performance of the stock price relative to the overall market. So, if the stock moves up 0.5% when the overall markets are up 1%, the rating would be below average (C being average). IBD updates the score daily, but it is based on the performance over the last 13 weeks.

What do you need to get started? Well, like in most other situations, you need the right tools for the job. And in investing this holds true as well. But, it's not as bad as you may think. Many of the tools/technical indicators used in the Perfect Storm System are available for free on several investing websites or on any trading platforms (if you have an account with them). The only tools that will require a subscription are the tools referenced from the Investor's Business Daily (IBD). However, IBD offers online access and a weekly print edition for less than $30 per month (at the time of this writing). Some sources to utilize are:

- Yahoo Finance: Stock Prices, Charts, and Option Pricing, Historical Stock Prices, Fundamental Information (EPS for previous quarters, Financial Statements, Analyst Estimates, etc…)
- Think or Swim (TD Ameritrade): Stock Prices, Charts, Options Prices as well a demo account option to practice your trading before risking any of your own money
- CBOE.com: Option Pricing information
- Stockcharts.com: Stock Charts, Average Directional Movement, Commodity Channel Index, Chaikin Money Flow, Price Momentum Oscillator, Prings Know Sure Things, Rate of Change, Stochastic and True Strength
- Investor's Business Daily (IBD): Market Trend, New Highs and Lows (NYSE, NASDAQ), Advancing Declining Issues, Market Volatility Index (VIX), Put/Call Premium Ratio, Bears vs. Bulls Ratio, Price Momentum (DOW, S&P, NASDAQ, GOLD)

A key to successful investing and trading is to never fall in love with a stock. Don't let your emotions over rule what the technical indicators are telling you. Make money while you can, but when the technical indicators turn, listen to them. The Perfect Storm System is designed to take a lot of the emotional aspects of investing and trading out of the equation. By remaining disciplined and understanding the tools in front of you, you will be able to develop a trading strategy that will be productive for you. This book will help you understand not only the components of the Perfect Storm System, but also tools for maximizing your return through the use of options. Together they can provide you years of successful investing/trading, no matter what direction the markets are moving.

Accumulation/Distribution

Formula

Accumulation/Distribution Line

(Close - Low) - (High - Close) / (High - Low) * Period's volume

Accumulation/distribution line was created by Marc Chalking to determine the flow of money into or out of a security (Investopedia).

Overview

The accumulation/ distribution is a momentum indicator that links changes in price and volume. The accumulation/distribution line is based on the principle that the more volume that is associated with a price

Interpretation

Accumulation Distribution can be used to find turning points in the market, which will be found when a divergence occurs. When the market makes a higher high but the accumulation distribution is lower than its

Example

The accumulation / distribution formula in the IBD, (investment business daily) is a quick and easy way to track a stock or index. There are five major levels of accumulation /distribution A, B, C, D, and E. The IBD has a price and volume formula that shows if a stock or index is under accumulation (buying) or distribution (selling) over the last 3 months. A, means buying and E, means selling. We can use this information as a daily signal as shown in the accumulation/distribution chart on the next page. We have a small example from 5/9/14 to 8/7/14; the trigger is when the accumulation/distribution changes and the index moves the opposite way, the next day. In this sample out of 23 time the formula was correct 16 time a success rate of 70%. The information can also be used as a trend indicator as shown in the accumulation/distribution chart on the next page. On 5/15/14 the S&P hit a low as did the accumulation/Distribution, (D-). As the index moved up the Accumulation/Distribution, moved up from a(D-) to a (B) and then at the high leveled off at a (B-) on 7/23/14. The market after hitting the high of 1987.01 then started to fade as did the Accumulation/Distribution, as the market faded from 1987.01 to 1909.57 on 8/7/14 the Accumulation/Distribution went from a (B-) to (D-). In the chart the up and down column is an easy way to track the trend movement of the accumulation / distribution in correlation with the close of the index. We never use one indicator, or one formula decide to invest or track the market always use multiple indicators and formulas to ensure a major trend and eliminate investing in a minor trend.

date	close	A/D	same	opposite	up	down
5/9/2014	1878.48	d+				
5/12/2014	1896.65	d		1		1
5/13/2014	1897.45	d				1
5/14/2014	1888.53	d+		1	1	
5/15/2014	1870.85	d-		1		1
5/16/2014	1877.86	d	1		1	
5/19/2014	1885.08	d			1	
5/20/2014	1872.83	d+	1			
5/21/2014	1888.03	d+			1	
5/22/2014	1892.49	d+			1	
5/23/2014	1900.53	d		1		1
5/27/2014	1911.97	c		1	1	
5/28/2014	1909.78	c-		1		1
5/29/2014	1920.03	c-				1
5/30/2014	1923.57	c	1		1	
6/2/2014	1924.97	c			1	
6/3/2014	1924.24	c			1	
6/4/2014	1927.88	c			1	
6/5/2014	1940.46	c+	1		1	
6/6/2014	1949.44	c+			1	
6/9/2014	1951.27	c+			1	
6/10/2014	1950.79	c+			1	
6/11/2014	1943.89	c+			1	
6/12/2014	1930.11	c		1		1
6/13/2014	1936.16	c				1
6/16/2014	1937.78	c				1
6/17/2014	1941.99	c+	1		1	
6/18/2014	1956.98	b-	1		1	
6/19/2014	1959.48	b-			1	
6/20/2014	1962.87	b-			1	
6/23/2014	1962.61	b-			1	
6/24/2014	1949.98	b-			1	
6/25/2014	1959.53	b-			1	
6/26/2004	1957.22	b-			1	
6/27/2014	1960.96	b		1	1	
6/30/2014	1960.23	b			1	
7/1/2014	1973.32	b			1	
7/2/2014	1974.62	b			1	
7/3/2014	1985.44	b			1	
7/7/2014	1977.65	b			1	
7/8/2014	1963.71	b-		1		1
7/9/2014	1972.83	b-				1
7/10/2014	1964.68	c+		1		1
7/11/2014	1967.51	c+				1
7/14/2014	1977.1	c+				1
7/15/2014	1973.28	c		1		1
7/16/2014	1981.57	b-		1	1	
7/17/2014	1958.12	c		1		1
7/18/2014	1978.22	b-		1	1	
7/21/2014	1973.63	b-			1	
7/22/2014	1983.53	b-			1	
7/23/2014	1987.01	b-			1	
7/24/2014	1987.98	b-			1	
7/25/2014	1978.34	b-			1	
7/28/2014	1978.91	b-			1	
7/29/2014	1969.91	c		1		1
7/30/2014	1970.07	c				1
7/31/2014	1929.8	d	1			1
8/1/2014	1925.15	d-		1		1
8/4/2014	1938.99	d-				1
8/5/2014	1920.21	d-				1
8/6/2014	1920.24	d-				1
8/7/2014	1909.57	d-				1

Arms Index

Formula

(advancing issues/declining issues) AD RATIO

(volume of advancing issues/volume of declining issues) AD VOLUME RATIO

(ad ratio/ad volume ratio) = TRIN

Developed in 1967 by Richard Arms, this volume-based breadth indicator can be applied over various time periods.

Overview

A technical analysis indicator that compares advancing and declining stock issues and trading volume as an indicator of overall market outlook. The Arms Index, or TRIN (Traders Index), is used as a predictor of future price movements in the market primarily daily.

Interpretation

The Arms Index value above one is bearish, a value below one is bullish and a value of one indicates a balanced market. Traders look not only at the value of the index, but also at how it changes. Any time there are extremes in the index value this is a sign that the market may soon change directions.

Example

On the next page we have two examples of the arms index. The first chart is the Nasdaq I like to use the arms index to track the Nasdaq and a separate table for the standard and Poor's 500 and the Dow. On the first chart on page, 8 you can see a section of a spread sheet that I track daily. The red color line across the page on 4/7/15 is the low of the Nasdaq for this time period. The green colored line on 4/27/15 is the high for the period. The column that is highlighted in red and green is the index trigger, for a buy or sell green is a call and red is a put. On 3/23/15 the arms index turned down one day after the market hit its high for the trend, and then the market turned down. On 4/6/15 the day before the market hit its low for the trend the arms index is showing a buy signal. Here The market is trend is changing faster than usual, but the arms index gives you a good insight on what the sentiment of the market.

As for the S&P and the Dow jones we track it the same way as the Nasdaq but we use the NYSE, numbers to calculate the arms index as shown on the chart on the next page. We use the same format as the Nasdaq and we use the same color coding. On page 8 we have a sample of how we track the issues. On the second chart, the NYSE is showing the markets hitting a high on 1/22/14 and on the next day the arms index is showing a sell signal as the market drops. On 1/30/14 the highlight area is showing the markets hit a low while the next day the arms index is showing a buy signal as the market moves up. On both charts I like to watch the advancing issues along with the advancing volume. On page 8 on 4/27/15 you can see the NASDAQ making a new high for the trend, while the advance issues, and volume are not advancing this is a red flag, and in this example the market changed direction. We never use one indicator or one formula to invest or track the market always use multiple indicators and formulas to ensure a major trend and eliminate investing in a minor trend.

	Close	ADV	DEC	ADV Vol	DEC Vol	Issues	Vol		UP	DOWN
3/20/2015	5026.42	1558	1115	1,690,309,000.00	819,539,000.00	1.40	2.06	0.68	1	0
3/23/2015	5010.97	1558	1288	670,581,000.00	852,727,000.00	1.21	0.79	1.54	0	1
3/24/2015	4994.73	1558	1410	617,710,000.00	929,420,000.00	1.10	0.66	1.66	0	1
3/25/2015	4876.52	1558	2237	334,163,000.00	1,754,113,000.00	0.70	0.19	3.66	0	1
3/26/2015	4863.36	1558	1487	825,778,000.00	1,077,880,000.00	1.05	0.77	1.37	0	1
3/27/2015	4891.22	1558	1101	1,034,958,000.00	558,218,000.00	1.42	1.85	0.76	1	0
3/30/2015	4947.44	1852	874	1,159,455,000.00	541,833,000.00	2.12	2.14	0.99	1	0
3/31/2015	4900.88	1086	1639	529,587,000.00	1,172,144,000.00	0.66	0.45	1.47	0	1
4/1/2015	4880.23	1275	1442	682,430,000.00	1,055,228,000.00	0.88	0.65	1.37	0	1
4/2/2015	4886.94	1636	1086	865,212,000.00	619,823,000.00	1.51	1.40	1.08	1	0
4/6/2015	4917.32	1499	1260	1,047,709,000.00	567,906,000.00	1.19	1.84	0.64	1	0
4/7/2015	4910.23	1266	1454	722,783,000.00	783,066,000.00	0.87	0.92	0.94	0	1
4/8/2015	4950.82	1734	972	1,114,284,000.00	512,131,000.00	1.78	2.18	0.82	1	0
4/9/2015	4974.56	1307	1389	1,015,921,000.00	652,111,000.00	0.94	1.56	0.60	1	0
4/10/2015	4995.98	1598	1098	981,068,000.00	470,668,000.00	1.46	2.08	0.70	1	0
4/13/2015	4988.25	1306	1401	684,366,000.00	801,006,000.00	0.93	0.85	1.09	0	1
4/14/2015	4977.29	1279	1416	689,659,000.00	835,841,000.00	0.90	0.83	1.09	0	1
4/15/2015	5011.22	1813	923	1,234,303,000.00	492,958,000.00	1.96	2.50	0.78	1	0
4/16/2015	5007.79	1277	1429	714,352,000.00	849,974,000.00	0.89	0.84	1.06	0	1
4/17/2015	4931.81	590	2154	364,869,000.00	1,549,825,000.00	0.27	0.24	1.16	0	1
4/21/2015	4994.60	1877	872	1,161,290,000.00	411,653,000.00	2.15	2.82	0.76	1	0
4/22/2015	5014.10	1339	1379	967,757,000.00	649,924,000.00	0.97	1.49	0.65	1	0
4/23/2015	5035.46	1478	1265	975,450,000.00	618,745,000.00	1.17	1.58	0.74	1	0
4/24/2015	5056.06	1652	1057	1,048,648,000.00	736,482,000.00	1.56	1.42	1.10	1	0
4/27/2015	5060.25	803	1953	647,618,000.00	1,362,082,000.00	0.41	0.48	0.86	1	0
4/28/2015	5055.42	1655	1062	1,021,772,000.00	930,439,000.00	1.56	1.10	1.42	0	1

nyse	dow	s&p	advancing	declining	advancing	declining	arms index			up	down
1/16/2015	17511.57	2019.42	2588	572	3,444,465,000.00	493,882,000.00	4.52	6.97	0.65	1	
1/20/2015	17515.23	2022.55	1227	1937	1,519,409,000.00	2,273,664,000.00	0.63	0.67	0.95	1	
1/21/2015	17554.28	2032.12	1996	1131	2,631,563,000.00	945,662,000.00	1.76	2.78	0.63	1	
1/22/2014	17813.38	2063.14	2460	687	3,251,394,000.00	770,082,000.00	3.58	4.22	0.85	1	
1/23/2015	17672.6	2051.82	1384	1722	1,118,780,000.00	2,316,847,000.00	0.80	0.48	1.66		1
1/26/2015	17678.7	2057.09	2150	982	2,397,801,000.00	887,250,000.00	2.19	2.70	0.81	1	
1/27/2015	17387.21	2029.55	1370	1757	1,155,326,000.00	2,033,366,000.00	0.78	0.57	1.37		1
1/28/2015	17191.37	2002.16	837	2340	400,100,000.00	3,545,872,000.00	0.36	0.11	3.17		1
1/29/2015	17416.85	2021.25	2116	1029	2,347,028,000.00	1,611,012,000.00	2.06	1.46	1.41		1
1/30/2015	17164.95	1994.99	1013	2159	1,202,537,000.00	3,172,330,000.00	0.47	0.38	1.24		1
2/2/2015	17361.04	2020.85	2298	854	3,148,374,000.00	716,293,000.00	2.69	4.40	0.61	1	
2/3/2015	17666.4	2022.71	2529	649	3,982,663,000.00	539,702,000.00	3.90	7.38	0.53	1	

Average Directional Movement

Formula

The ADX was originally developed by J. Welles Wilder and published in his book New Concepts in Technical Trading Systems, June 1978. Go to stock charts.com to view this formula it is too complicated to lay it out in this book.

Overview

The Average Directional Index (ADX) is used to measure the strength and weakness of a trend, not the actual direction. Directional movement is defined by +DI and –DI. In general, the bulls have the edge when +DI is greater than – DI, while the bears have the edge when – DI is greater. Crosses of these directional indicators can be combined with ADX for triggers when the direction strength is fading

Interpretation

At its most basic the Average Directional Index (ADX) can be used to determine if a security is trending or not. This helps traders choose between a trend following system or a non-trend following system.

Wilder suggests that a strong trend is present when ADX is above 25 and no trend is present when below 20. When the issue is between 20 and 25 this is a neutral area. You can adjust the settings to increase sensitivity and signals. ADX also has a good amount of lag because of all the smoothing in the system. Many technical analysts use 20 as the key level for ADX.

Example

The average directional movement can be a little complicated, so I added a few simple convergence/divergence formulas with color, to make it easy to see the direction of each move, the ADX itself and the fast and slow movement. On the chart on the next page you can see an example of the NASDAQ from 11/10/14 to 1/15/15. The third column is the change of the ADX from the previous day,(the forth column) the green color is when the ADX is moving in a upwards direction and the red color is when the ADX is running in a downward direction. The fifth column (f) is the c/d of the seventh column (fast or plus column) and the ADX in the green color means the fast column (7) is higher than the ADX column (4) and when the column turns red it means the (fast or plus column) is lower than the ADX column (4). The s column works the same way as the f column the green color means the s or minus column (8) is higher than the ADX column (4) and when the column turns red that means the s or minus column is lower than the ADX column (4). The c/d column (9) is the convergence / divergence of the fast (7) and slow (8) column, when the column is green that means the fast or plus (7) is higher than the slow or minus column (8).

    The key to any formula is understanding, the indicators, and there are two indicators, I use when working with the average directional movement formula. The first indicator and most important indicator is the ADX line this is the key to the strength of the move column (3). Then second indicator is the c/d column (9), this tells us the direction of the move. The trigger is when the ADX c/d column (3) and the c/d column (9) are moving together. For example,6t on the chart on page 10 you can see on 11/10/14 the c/d ADX column (3) is moving up as well at the c/d column (9) until 12/1/15 when c/d ADX column (3) runs out of strength as does the c/d column (9) on 12/9/14 as the NASDAQ hit its low on 12/16/14 for the move. For a down trend we are looking for the c/d ADX column (3) to move up while the c/d column (9) is moving down this would be a trigger for a down trend. We never use one indicator or one formula to invest or track the market always use multiple indicators and formulas to insure a major trend and eliminate investing in a minor trend.

date	close	c/d adx	adx	f	s	fast	slow	c/d	up	down
11/10/2014	4651.62	0.34	25.8	4.75	-9.42	30.55	16.38	14.17	1	
11/11/2014	4660.56	0.43	26.23	4.51	-10.31	30.74	15.92	14.82	1	
11/12/2014	4675.78	0.64	26.87	4.78	-11.71	31.65	15.16	16.49	1	
11/13/2014	4679.85	1.1	27.97	4.96	-13.35	32.93	14.62	18.31	1	
11/14/2014	4688.54	0.7	28.67	3.51	-14.85	32.18	13.82	18.36	1	
11/17/2014	4671	0.5	29.17	1.37	-14.7	30.54	14.47	16.07	1	
11/18/2014	4702.44	0.77	29.94	41.87	-16.31	71.81	13.63	58.18	1	
11/19/2014	4694.78	0.15	30.09	-1.51	-14.94	28.58	15.15	13.43	1	
11/20/2014	4701.87	0.16	30.25	-1.87	-15.94	28.38	14.31	14.07	1	
11/21/2014	4712.97	0.94	31.19	2	-17.97	33.19	13.22	19.97	1	
11/24/2014	4754.89	0.92	32.11	-0.23	-19.72	31.88	12.39	19.49	1	
11/25/2014	4758.25	1.12	33.23	0.47	-21.32	33.7	11.91	21.79	1	
11/26/2014	4787.32	1.21	34.44	-0.23	-23.11	34.21	11.33	22.88	1	
11/28/2014	4791.63	1.41	35.85	0.78	-24.97	36.63	10.88	25.75	1	
12/1/2014	4727.35	-0.77	35.08	-2.36	-15.48	32.72	19.6	13.12	1	
12/2/2014	4755.81	-0.71	34.37	-3.46	-15.86	30.91	18.51	12.4	1	
12/3/2014	4774.47	-0.31	34.06	-1.75	-16.65	32.31	17.41	14.9	1	
12/4/2014	4769.44	-0.06	34	-4.23	-17.77	29.77	16.23	13.54	1	
12/5/2014	4780.75	-0.19	33.81	-2.98	-17.88	30.83	15.93	14.9	1	
12/8/2014	4740.69	-1.53	32.28	-5.04	-10.48	27.24	21.8	5.44	1	
12/9/2014	4766.46	-2.09	30.19	-6.86	-4.11	23.33	26.08	-2.75		1
12/10/2014	4684.03	-1.76	28.43	-8.03	-5.62	20.4	22.81	-2.41		1
12/11/2014	4708.16	-1.63	26.8	-8.54	-6.39	18.26	20.41	-2.15		1
12/12/2014	4653.6	-0.51	26.29	-9.41	-1.09	16.88	25.2	-8.32		1
12/15/2014	4575.74	-0.02	26.27	-12.48	3.35	13.79	29.62	-15.83		1
12/16/2014	4547.83	1.67	27.94	-14.98	3.93	12.96	31.87	-18.91		1
12/17/2014	4644.31	0.82	28.76	-16.58	-0.75	12.18	28.01	-15.83		1
12/18/2014	4748.4	-1.54	27.22	-5.76	-2.44	21.46	24.78	-3.32		1
12/19/2014	4738.29	-1.85	25.37	-1.15	-1.82	24.22	23.55	0.67	1	
12/22/2014	4781.42	-1.71	23.66	-0.13	-0.79	23.53	22.87	0.66	1	
12/23/2014	4765.42	-1.29	22.37	2.07	-0.52	24.44	21.85	2.59	1	
12/24/2014	4773.47	-1.2	21.17	2.58	0.06	23.75	21.23	2.52	1	
12/26/2014	4806.86	-0.59	20.58	5.45	-0.49	26.03	20.09	5.94	1	
12/29/2014	4806.91	-0.35	20.23	5.27	-0.55	25.5	19.68	5.82	1	
12/30/2014	4777.44	-1.34	18.89	5.39	3.51	24.28	22.4	1.88	1	
12/31/2014	4736.05	-0.76	18.13	3.55	6.75	21.68	24.88	-3.2		1
1/2/2014	4726.81	-0.13	18	1.61	9.58	19.61	27.58	-7.97		1
1/5/2014	4652.57	0.78	18.78	-1.29	12.99	17.49	31.77	-14.28		1
1/6/2015	4592.74	1.59	20.37	-4.98	16.46	15.39	36.83	-21.44		1
1/7/2015	4650.47	1.48	21.85	-7.56	12.33	14.29	34.18	-19.89		1
1/8/2015	4736.19	-0.56	21.29	1.74	9.3	23.03	30.59	-7.56		1
1/9/2015	4704.07	-0.42	20.87	0.48	8.26	21.35	29.13	-7.78		1
1/12/2015	4664.71	0.04	20.91	-1.16	9.55	19.75	30.46	-10.71		1
1/13/2015	4661.5	-0.67	20.24	0.63	6.08	20.87	26.32	-5.45		1
1/14/2015	4639.32	-0.21	20.03	-0.63	7.48	19.4	27.51	-8.11		1
1/15/2015	4570.82	0.19	20.22	-2.76	7.5	17.46	27.72	-10.26		1

BOLLINGER BANDS

Formula

Middle band = 20 day simple moving average (SMA)

Upper band = 20 day sma + (20 day standard deviation of price x 2)

Lower band = 20 day sma − (20 day standard deviation of price x 2)

"Developed by John Bollinger, Bollinger Bands® are volatility bands placed above and below a moving average. Volatility is based on the standard deviation, which changes as volatility increases and decreases".

Overview

The Bollinger Bands automatically widen when volatility increases and narrow when volatility decreases. This dynamic nature of Bollinger Bands also means they can be used on different securities with the standard settings for signals. Bollinger Bands can be used to identify Tops and Bottoms or to determine the strength of the trend.

Interpretation

Bollinger Bands mirror direction with the 20-period SMA and volatility with the upper/lower bands. They can be used to determine if prices are relatively high or low. According to Bollinger, the Bands should contain 80% of the price action, which makes a move outside the bands noteworthy. prices are generally, high when above the upper band and relatively low when below the lower band. A relatively high signal should not be viewed as bearish or as a sell signal. Likewise, relatively low signal should not be considered bullish or as a buy signal. Prices are high or low for a reason. As with other indicators, Bollinger Bands are not meant to be used as a standalone tool. we should combine Bollinger Bands with basic trend analysis and other indicators for confirmation, be for we make our move.

Example

On the next page there is an example of my formula using the Bollinger Band figures for the NASDAQ. I use the high and low Bollinger Band numbers to calculate the movement of an index or issue.

The Convergence/Divergence (c/d) column is the trigger of the formula. The last two column are the motion of the movement of the index using this formula, either up or down. On the chart on the next page you can see how when the index hits its high on 9/17/15 and 11/3/15 the same day or the next day the formula is telling us that the move is at the end and the direction of the trend has changed. On 9/29/15 you can see how the index hit the low of the trend, as shown in the formula and the next day the formula shows us a run up eight out of nine days for a 321 point move up in the short term, and a 628 point move until the trend is over on 11/3/15. This formula is more sensitive than using the convergence/ divergence of the Bollinger Band you can see in the chart this formula changes faster to provide a bottom or a top more accurately. There is another signal to watch. 10/28/15 you can see two highlighted areas under the high minus close and c/d minus h/l c/d. Both areas are highlighted in red and are showing negative numbers this means that the numbers are outside the Bollinger Bands and outside the Bollinger Band c/d minus the close high low c/d. This is a signal that the market should go down as it did the next day.

When viewing the chart below you can clearly see the strength of the direction of the move in column 12 (C/D the trigger) as the c/d drops or moves higher so goes the index. We never use one indicator or one formula to invest or track the market always use multiple indicators and formulas to ensure a major trend and eliminate investing in a minor trend.

CONNELLY FORMULA USING BOLLINGER BANDS DATA

DATE	CLOSE	Bollinger Bands High	low	Convergence/ Divergence	high minus close	close minus low	high low close c/d	c/d BB minus h/l c/d	BB/cd-(high-close+h l c/d)	(close-low+hlclos e c/d)-bb c/d	Convergence/D ivergence	up	down
9/17/2015	4,893.93	4,970.18	4,546.96	423.22	76.23	346.99	270.76	152.46	76.23	194.53	118.30	1	0
9/18/2015	4,827.23	4,963.10	4,549.01	414.09	135.87	278.22	142.35	271.74	135.87	6.48	(129.39)	0	1
9/21/2015	4,828.96	4,970.24	4,554.16	416.08	141.28	274.80	133.52	282.56	141.28	(7.76)	(149.04)	0	1
9/22/2015	4,756.72	4,951.55	4,595.90	355.65	194.83	160.82	(34.01)	389.66	194.83	(228.84)	(423.67)	0	1
9/23/2015	4,752.74	4,915.72	4,656.30	259.42	162.98	96.44	(66.54)	325.96	162.98	(229.52)	(392.50)	1	0
9/24/2015	4,734.48	4,913.46	4,662.30	251.16	178.98	72.18	(106.80)	357.96	178.98	(285.78)	(464.76)	0	1
9/25/2015	4,686.50	4,914.05	4,649.12	264.93	227.55	37.38	(190.17)	455.10	227.55	(417.72)	(645.27)	0	1
9/28/2015	4,543.97	4,933.46	4,601.26	332.20	389.49	(57.29)	(446.78)	778.98	389.49	(836.27)	(1,225.76)	0	1
9/29/2015	4,517.32	4,952.90	4,555.89	397.01	435.58	(38.57)	(474.15)	871.16	435.58	(909.73)	(1,345.31)	0	1
9/30/2015	4,620.17	4,954.12	4,553.08	401.04	333.95	67.09	(266.86)	667.90	333.95	(600.81)	(934.76)	1	0
10/1/2015	4,627.28	4,955.43	4,539.48	415.95	328.15	87.80	(240.35)	656.30	328.15	(568.50)	(896.65)	1	0
10/2/2015	4,707.77	4,955.43	4,539.48	415.95	247.66	168.29	(79.37)	495.32	247.66	(327.03)	(574.69)	1	0
10/5/2015	4,781.26	4,958.16	4,543.91	414.25	176.90	237.35	60.45	353.80	176.90	(116.45)	(293.35)	1	0
10/6/2015	4,748.36	4,953.09	4,542.63	410.46	204.73	205.73	1.00	409.46	204.73	(203.73)	(408.46)	0	1
10/7/2015	4,791.15	4,955.67	4,543.51	412.16	164.52	247.64	83.12	329.04	164.52	(81.40)	(245.92)	1	0
10/8/2015	4,810.79	4,957.15	4,543.48	413.67	146.36	267.31	120.95	292.72	146.36	(25.41)	(171.77)	1	0
10/9/2015	4,830.47	4,958.15	4,543.30	414.85	127.68	287.17	159.49	255.36	127.68	31.81	(95.87)	1	0
10/12/2015	4,838.64	4,962.02	4,542.71	419.31	123.38	295.93	172.55	246.76	123.38	49.17	(74.21)	1	0
10/13/2015	4,796.61	4,954.03	4,544.31	409.72	157.42	252.30	94.88	314.84	157.42	(62.54)	(219.96)	0	1
10/14/2015	4,782.85	4,939.19	4,548.52	390.67	156.34	234.33	77.99	312.68	156.34	(78.35)	(234.69)	0	1
10/15/2015	4,870.10	4,934.58	4,550.74	383.84	64.48	319.36	254.88	128.96	64.48	190.40	125.92	1	0
10/16/2015	4,886.69	4,946.27	4,546.75	399.52	59.58	339.94	280.36	119.16	59.58	220.78	161.20	1	0
10/19/2015	4,905.47	4,957.25	4,541.66	415.59	51.78	363.81	312.03	103.56	51.78	260.25	208.47	1	0
10/20/2015	4,880.97	4,971.24	4,540.10	431.14	90.27	340.87	250.60	180.54	90.27	160.33	70.06	0	1
10/21/2015	4,840.12	4,978.72	4,541.36	437.36	138.60	298.76	160.16	277.20	138.60	21.56	(117.04)	0	1
10/22/2015	4,920.05	4,998.37	4,540.26	458.11	78.32	379.79	301.47	156.64	78.32	223.15	144.83	1	0
10/23/2015	5,031.86	5,038.95	4,534.22	504.73	7.09	497.64	490.55	14.18	7.09	483.46	476.37	1	0
10/26/2015	5,034.70	5,059.76	4,562.49	497.27	25.06	472.21	447.15	50.12	25.06	422.09	397.03	0	1
10/27/2015	5,030.15	5,063.74	4,609.78	453.96	33.59	420.37	386.78	67.18	33.59	353.19	319.60	0	1
10/28/2015	5,095.69	5,091.37	4,623.71	467.66	(4.32)	471.98	476.30	(8.64)	(4.32)	480.62	484.94	1	0
10/29/2015	5,074.27	5,105.43	4,660.37	445.06	31.16	413.90	382.74	62.32	31.16	351.58	320.42	0	1
10/30/2015	5,053.75	5,119.35	4,681.05	438.30	65.60	372.70	307.10	131.20	65.60	241.50	175.90	0	1
11/2/2015	5,127.15	5,150.52	4,684.46	466.06	23.37	442.69	419.32	46.74	23.37	395.95	372.58	1	0
11/3/2015	5,145.13	5,176.85	4,697.81	479.04	31.72	447.32	415.60	63.44	31.72	383.88	352.16	0	1
11/4/2015	5,142.48	5,200.42	4,709.38	491.04	57.94	433.10	375.16	115.88	57.94	317.22	259.28	0	1
11/5/2015	5,127.74	5,217.92	4,723.56	494.36	90.18	404.18	314.00	180.36	90.18	223.82	133.64	0	1
11/6/2015	5,147.12	5,236.34	4,736.81	499.53	89.22	410.31	321.09	178.44	89.22	231.87	142.65	1	0
11/9/2015	5,095.30	5,243.77	4,755.05	488.72	148.47	340.25	191.78	296.94	148.47	43.31	(105.16)	0	1
11/10/2015	5,083.24	5,241.93	4,785.56	456.37	158.69	297.68	138.99	317.38	158.69	(19.70)	(178.39)	0	1
11/11/2015	5,067.02	5,230.84	4,825.06	405.78	163.82	241.96	78.14	327.64	163.82	(85.68)	(249.50)	0	1
11/12/2015	5,005.08	5,224.71	4,844.68	380.03	219.63	160.40	(59.23)	439.26	219.63	(278.86)	(498.49)	0	1
11/13/2015	4,927.88	5,221.12	4,852.40	368.72	293.24	75.48	(217.76)	586.48	293.24	(511.00)	(804.24)	0	1

Bulls Vs. Bears

Formula

Bull verse bear ratio=bullish investment advisors/bearish investment advisors.
　　Bull verse bear ratio= bull / (bull +bear) *100.

Overview

A market sentiment indicator published weekly by investor's intelligence that uses information polled directly from market professionals. This index reflects the sentiments of market participants that deal daily with the financial markets and it gives a more relevant measure. Investopedia.com

Interpretation

High readings of the ratio indicate a bearish sentiment, whereas low readings indicate bullish one. Typically, extreme high and low readings have shown markets reaching, tops and bottoms.

Example

My favorite paper is the Investor's Business Daily the IBD, I pull my daily bull verse bear ratio from the IBD every morning. I like to do a few things with this information I track the signal, when the convergence and divergence of the bull verse bear numbers changes that is a signal to buy or sell. How we track the bull bear percentage is simply minus the bull percentage from the bear percentage, this is different from the standard formula listed above, but I find this to be a simple way to stay on the right side of the market. On the chart on the next page you can see, as the convergence and divergence of the bull, bear percentages change in direction the NASDAQ follow soon after. Never use one formula or signal to make a transaction.

Date	bull	bear	
2/18/2015	56.6	14.1	42.5
2/19/2015	56.6	14.1	42.5
2/20/2015	56.6	14.1	42.5
2/23/2014	56.6	14.1	42.5
2/24/2015	56.6	14.1	42.5
2/25/2015	59.5	14.1	45.4
2/26/2015	59.5	14.1	45.4
2/27/2015	59.5	14.1	45.4
3/2/2014	59.5	14.1	45.4
3/3/2015	59.5	14.1	45.4
3/4/2015	59.5	14.1	45.4
3/5/2015	59.7	14.1	45.6
3/6/2015	58.7	14.1	44.6
3/9/2015	58.7	14.1	44.6
3/10/2015	58.7	14.1	44.6
3/11/2015	53.6	14.1	39.5
3/12/2015	53.6	14.1	39.5
3/13/2015	53.6	14.1	39.5
3/16/2015	53.6	14.1	39.5

Chaiken Money Flow

Formula

The following is the formula for the Chaikin Money Flow Indicator:

> Step 1: ((Close – Low) – (High – Close)/ (High – Low)) * Volume
>
> Step 2: 21 Day Average of Step1 (Daily MF) / 21 Day Average of Volume"

Chaiken power tools .com

Overview

With the Chaiken Money Flow we are computing a one-day net positive or negative money flow based on whether a stock closes above or below its' mid-point for the day, measuring how close to its' high or low it is at the close, and then relating that to the volume.

Interpretation

The Chaiken Money Flow measures the flow of funds into and out of a stock over a, one-month time period. Each day's trading pattern is analyzed to arrive at a net accumulation/distribution number. The key to the value of this approach is the observation that strong stocks tend to close in the upper portion of their range, day in and day out, and on rising volume. Volume is the energy that powers markets and stock price movement.

Example

On the next page you can see an example of the Chaiken Money Flow at work. The chart is based of the Nasdaq, the column marked Chaiken Money Flow is highlighted in red and green, red meaning bearish down and green meaning bullish up. On 4/11/14 you can see the Nasdaq hit a low, as the chaiken money flow hit its low of -159, and as the issue started to move up so did the Chaiken Money Flow. Over the course of forty days the chaiken money flow went form a minus 159 to a positive 276, during this time the Nasdaq went from 3999.73 to 4237.07 for a move of 237.34 points. We never just use one indicator to invest in the market. We never use one indicator or one formula to invest or track the market always use multiple indicators and formulas to ensure a major trend and eliminate investing in a minor trend.

Date	CLOSE	Chaiken Money Flow
4/9/2014	4183.90	0.146
4/10/2014	4054.11	-0.157
4/11/2014	3999.73	-0.159
4/14/2014	4022.69	-0.133
4/15/2014	4034.16	-0.142
4/16/2014	4086.23	-0.097
4/17/2014	4095.52	-0.102
4/21/2014	4121.55	-0.017
4/22/2014	4161.46	0.22
4/23/2014	4126.97	-0.009
4/24/2014	4148.34	0.58
4/25/2014	4075.56	0.036
4/28/2014	4074.40	0.079
4/29/2014	4103.54	0.101
4/30/2014	4114.56	0.097
5/1/2014	4127.45	0.081
5/2/2014	4123.9	0.080
5/5/2014	4138.06	0.161
5/6/2014	4080.76	0.155
5/7/2014	4067.67	0.134
5/8/2014	4051.5	0.054
5/9/2014	4071.87	0.147
5/12/2014	4143.86	0.235
5/13/2014	4130.17	0.161
5/14/2014	4100.63	0.126
5/15/2014	4069.29	0.082
5/16/2014	4090.59	0.109
5/19/2014	4125.81	0.106
5/20/2014	4096.89	0.097
5/21/2014	4131.54	0.148
5/22/2014	4154.34	0.157
5/23/2014	4185.81	0.239
5/27/2014	4237.07	0.276

THE COMMODITY CHANNEL INDEX

Formula

"The CCI is calculated by first finding the typical price for the period TP, which is one third of the sum of the high, the low, and the close for the period. The average mean deviation in the typical prices, MDTP, is calculated for over n periods, as is the mean of the typical prices, MATP. The CCI is then defined as cci= (tp-matp)/ (0.15xmdtp)" (Advfn www, advfn.com)

Overview

"You can adjust the period over which the means are generated, and you can also select modified CCI, in which the typical price is calculated as one third of the sum of the close for the current period plus the highest high and the lowest low in n periods." (Advfn www, advfn.com)

"CCI generates a buy signal, when it crosses from below 100 to above -100. Similarly, it generates a sell signal, when it crosses from above 100 to below -100." (Advfn www, advfn.com).

Interpretation

"Developed by Donald Lambert and featured in Commodities magazine in 1980, the Commodity Channel Index (CCI) is a versatile indicator that can be used to identify a new trend or warn of extreme conditions. Lambert originally developed CCI to identify cyclical turns in commodities, but the indicator can successfully have applied to indices, ETFs, stocks and other securities. In general, CCI measures the current price level relative to an average price level over a given period. CCI is relatively high when prices are far above their average. CCI is relatively low when prices are far below their average. In this manner, CCI can be used to identify overbought and oversold levels." (Stock charts.com)

Example

The commodity channel index chart, on the next page gives us a view of the cci in action. The highlighted areas in red are the lows of the Dow and the green areas are the high of the DOW during this time frame. During this time frame the market is moving very quickly from tops to bottoms. The CCI can be used to help keep us on the right side of the market. The commodity channel index is a fast moving indicator that generally provides signals prior to most other indicators.

date	dow	cci	up	down
3/24/2015	18011.14	21.85	1	
3/25/2015	17718.54	-75.59	1	
3/26/2015	17678.23	-132.5	1	
3/27/2015	17712.66	-11.09	1	
3/30/2015	17976.48	-9.13	1	
3/31/2015	17776.12	-35.44	1	
4/1/2015	17698.18	-104.5	1	
4/2/2015	17763.24	-64.26	1	
4/6/2015	17880.85	-20.38	1	
4/7/2015	17875.42	31.85	1	
4/8/2015	17902.51	22.76		1
4/9/2015	17958.73	30.16	1	
4/10/2015	18057.65	86.13	1	
4/13/2015	17977.84	77.43	1	
4/14/2015	18036.7	62.61	1	
4/15/2015	18112.61	109.31		1
4/16/2015	18105.77	101.65		1
4/17/2015	17826.3	-14.99	1	
4/21/2015	18034.93	43.5	1	
4/22/2015	17949.59	55.55	1	
4/23/2015	18038.27	57.32	1	
4/24/2015	18058.69	85.57	1	
4/27/2015	18037	87.67	1	
4/28/2015	18110.14			1
4/29/2015	18035			1
4/30/2015	17840.52			1

Call/Put Volume & Open Interest

Formula

Calls divided by the puts and the call open interest divided the put open interest.

For the total calls/puts we also do a 10 day moving average using the same formula.

Overview

The calls / puts, is simply the amount of calls in one day, and the amount of puts in one day, and the open interest associated with both the calls and puts for the day.

Interpretation

The calls / puts volume is the amount of calls and puts being bought and sold for that specific day. The calls / puts open interest is also known as open contracts. Several technical analysts believe that a spike in open interest is usually due to some vital information revealed. Open interest increases in the market, can indicate that new money is flowing into the market. Open interest moving up or down does not mean the issues or market will go up or down. When open interest starts to level off after an issue has been rising for a good amount of time this could be a warning sign that the issue may be at the end of the uptrend.

Example

On the next page we have an example of calls/puts open interest formula, using a 10day moving average. The horizontal green and red lines are the high and low of the indexes, for that time frame. The vertical green and red areas in the C/D section (convergence/divergence) are when the calls are high then the 10 day (green) or red when the puts are higher than the 10 day moving average. The total call/put column and the 10day C/D column work the same way when the area is in green this means there are more calls then there are puts, and when it is red that means there are more puts then calls. The trigger for this formula is the 10 day moving average column, the 10 day average smooths the movement to give you a more accurate view of the indexes. As you can see in the chart on the next page. On 12/30/15 the indexes hit their high and on 1/4/16 the 10 day C/D is signaled the indexes are going to move down. The daily total call/put a down signal to 1/15/16. The 10 day signal then switched to positive on 1/19/16 a day prior to the market bottom for the period. We never use one indicator or one formula to invest or track the market always use multiple indicators and formulas to insure a major trend and eliminate investing in a minor trend.

Call Put Open Interest Formula

Date	DOW	S&P	Nasdaq	totals call	10day	c/d	open intrest	put	10 day	c/d	open intrest	total call/put	total interest call/put	up	down	10dayc/d
12/30/2015	17603.87	2063.36	5065.85	3003872	5267997	0.57	156067217	2693018	4585496	0.59	141919316	1.12	1.10			-0.02
12/31/2015	17425.03	2043.94	5007.41	4047123	5306657	0.76	157371950	3950367	4675733	0.84	143278803	1.02	1.10	1		-0.08
1/4/2016	17148.94	2012.66	4903.09	5315112	5101198	1.04	158337149	5494909	4670231	1.18	143951543	0.97	1.10		1	-0.13
1/5/2016	17158.66	2016.71	4891.43	4328829	4888387	0.89	156641758	5566412	4495282	0.92	142554745	1.05	1.10			-0.03
1/6/2016	16906.51	1990.26	4835.77	5307318	4705478	1.13	158823915	5550007	4274505	1.30	144453411	0.96	1.10	1		-0.17
1/7/2016	16514.1	1943.09	4689.43	7132051	4966491	1.44	161576142	9256059	4815313	1.92	147094645	0.77	1.10	1		-0.49
1/8/2016	16346.45	1922.03	4643.63	5683184	5121525	1.11	165904255	7366752	5186447	1.42	150783901	0.77	1.10	1		-0.31
1/11/2016	16398.57	1923.67	4637.99	6246547	5262387	1.19	168807054	6895304	5503481	1.25	151223664	0.91	1.12	1		-0.07
1/12/2016	16516.22	1938.68	4685.92	5652558	5343851	1.06	167806325	5812464	5712232	1.02	151537988	0.97	1.11		1	0.04
1/13/2016	16151.41	1890.28	4526.06	5907212	5639696	1.05	171116324	6809987	6099637	1.12	153942408	0.87	1.11	1		-0.07
1/14/2016	16379.05	1921.84	4615	7683495	6030730	1.27	174594011	8263735	6621048	1.25	156458471	0.93	1.12	1		0.03
1/15/2016	15988.08	1880.33	4488.42	8128561	6543199	1.24	178246428	11282212	7479967	1.51	158753789	0.72	1.12	1		-0.27
1/19/2016	16016.02	1881.33	4476.95	5765082	6714995	0.86	177114034	5145791	7599510	0.68	123180111	1.12	1.44		1	0.18
1/20/2016	15766.74	1859.33	4471.69	7737428	6957237	1.11	102800828	9102026	7960721	1.14	100592275	0.85	1.02			-0.03
1/21/2016	15882.68	1868.99	4472.06	5417687	7066112	0.77	106749360	5358567	8084290	0.66	105151177	1.01	1.02	1		0.10
1/22/2016	16093.51	1906.9	4591.18	5849700	7120351	0.82	108876749	5787013	8107991	0.71	107065743	1.01	1.02	1		0.11
1/25/2015	15885.22	1877.08	4518.49	3751875	6782333	0.55	110664624	3870039	7569389	0.51	109202498	0.97	1.01		1	0.04
1/26/2016	16167.23	1903.63	4503.52	4499569	6663971	0.68	109493608	3605249	7193239	0.50	107914218	1.25	1.01	1		0.17
1/27/2016	15944.46	1882.95	4468.17	5287967	6568113	0.81	112691357	4593904	6963099	0.66	110183211	1.15	1.02	1		0.15
1/28/2016	16069.64	1893.36	4506.68	6328978	6635755	0.95	115675491	4680350	6849887	0.68	112922613	1.35	1.02	1		0.27
1/29/2016	16466.3	1940.24	4613.95	8671963	6912231	1.25	118714979	6008217	6769710	0.89	115467120	1.44	0.10	1		0.37
2/1/2016	16449.18	1939.38	4620.37	4244507	6568332	0.65	119737036	3838976	6272234	0.61	117375666	1.11	1.02	1		0.04
2/2/2016	16153.54	1903.03	4516.95	4244507	6179926	0.69	120832143	5552726	5582911	0.69	117457192	1.11	1.02		1	0.00
2/3/2016	16336.66	1912.53	4504.24	6479850	6251403	1.04	120832143	5552726	5623604	0.99	117457192	1.17	1.03	1		0.05
2/4/2016	16416.58	1915.45	4509.56	5740017	6051662	0.95	124382814	5463087	5259710	1.04	120205122	1.05	1.03		1	-0.09
2/5/2016	16204.97	1880.05	4363.14	6576959	6167589	1.07	117858822	6555695	5377423	1.22	111358869	1.00	1.06			-0.15
2/8/2016	16027.05	1853.44	4283.75	6377427	6220362	1.03	129635080	7189837	5519706	1.30	124956336	0.89	1.04		1	-0.28
2/9/2016	16014.38	1852.21	4268.76	5499173	6395092	0.86	128366009	5679297	5700631	1.00	125732205	0.97	1.02		1	-0.14
2/10/2016	15914.74	1851.86	4283.59	5744822	5519617	1.04	131243904	2574711	5597578	0.46	125676412	2.23	1.04	1		0.42
2/11/2016	15660.18	1829.08	4266.84	7003852	6691706	1.05	133578	6860731	5824260	1.18	129411872	1.02	0.00	1		-0.13
2/12/2016	15973.84	1864.78	4337.51	6105231	6668831	0.92	137396147	5356592	5891885	0.91	130055441	1.14	1.06			0.01

FIBONACCI

Formula

When technical analyzing the market or issue, the Fibonacci retracement is generated by taking the peak and trough of an issue (high and low) and multiplying the vertical distance (subtract the high and low) by the key Fibonacci ratios of, 23.6% 38.2% 50% 61.8% 100% 1.618% 2.618% 4.236%.

Overview

For reasons that are unclear, these ratios seem to play an important role in the stock market, just as they do in nature, and can be used to determine critical points that cause an asset's price to reverse. The direction of the prior trend is likely to continue once the price of the asset has retraced to one of the ratios listed above. The following chart illustrates how Fibonacci retracement can be used. Notice how the price changes direction as it approaches the support/resistance levels. Investopedia.com

Interpretation

Leonardo Fibonacci was a mathematician from Italy, who died over 750 years ago. He discovered what we know as the Fibonacci sequence of numbers, where each number is the sum of the previous two numbers 1,1,2,3,5,8,13,21,34,55,89,144,ect. The numbers technical analyst use are called the Fibonacci retracement points or the golden ratio, 23.6% 38.2% 50% 61.8% 100%. All stock or issue generally rise and then pull back, regularly the issue will pivot closely to the Fibonacci retracement levels. By tracking these pivot points, it can indicate a good time to buy or sell a stock or index.

Example

On the chart on the next page you can see an example of the Fibonacci retracement in action. The first step is finding the high and low of the market, we have an example of the Dow jones in the chart on the next page, the high was on 5/19/15, 18,312.39 (in green) and the low was on 6/9/15 17764.04 (in red). The next step is calculating the difference of the two numbers this is the move or indicator (548.35). I also like to track the number of day elapsed between the high and low, in this case it was 14 days, which is faster than an average market move, this is something to keep an eye on we will get into market movement later in the book. Next step is to take the difference from the high and low and times it by the Fibonacci numbers as you can see in the chart on the next page, (548.35 x 0.236=129.41). The next step is to take the Fibonacci calculation and add it to the low of the index, that will give you your first retracement number (17764.04 + 129.41=17893.45) and so on until you complete all of the Fibonacci numbers, as you can see on the chart on the next page, I like to use .236 to 4.236 for my calculations. The Fibonacci can be used to track the markets moves up or down, no one formula can predict the movement of a stock or index. We never use one indicator or one formula to invest or track the market always use multiple indicators and formulas to ensure a major trend and eliminate investing in a minor trend.

Date	Value
5/19/2015	18,312.39
5/20/2015	18,285.40
5/21/2015	18,285.74
5/22/2015	18,232.02
5/26/2015	18,041.54
5/27/2015	18,162.99
5/28/2015	18,126.12
5/29/2015	18,010.68
6/1/2019	18,040.37
6/2/2019	18,011.94
6/3/2019	18,076.27
6/4/2019	17,905.58
6/5/2019	17,849.46
6/8/2019	17,766.55
6/9/2019	17,764.04
6/10/2019	18,000.40
6/11/2019	18,039.37
6/12/2019	17,898.84
6/15/2019	17,791.17
6/16/2019	17,904.48
6/17/2019	17,935.74
6/18/2019	18,115.84
6/19/2019	18,015.95
6/22/2019	18,119.78
6/23/2019	18,144.04

Fibonacci Numbers

			Days 14		
5/19/2015	18,312.39		0.236	129.41	17,893.45
6/9/2019	17,764.04		0.382	209.47	17,973.51
Move	548.35		0.5	274.18	18,038.22
			0.618	338.88	18,102.92
			1	548.35	18,312.39
			1.618	887.23	18,651.27
			2.618	1,435.58	19,199.62
			4.236	2,322.81	20,086.85

52 Week High 52 Week Low Formula

Formula

The 52 week high and the 52 week low index that I use is calculated by dividing the stocks that are making new 52 week highs by the stocks that are making new 52 week low's and then taking a 10 day average of the daily number, I do this for both the NYSE and the NASDAQ. The next step is to take the daily NYSE and the NASDAQ and compare them to each other (NYSE/Nasdaq) and do the same for the 10 day average (NYSE/Nasdaq).

Overview

An index that seeks to provide confirmation of a market trend by comparing the daily number of stocks reaching new 52-week highs with the number reaching new 52-week lows on a broad equity index. The high-low index is considered bullish if it is positive and rising and bearish if it is negative and falling. Since the index can be quite volatile on a day-to-day basis, market technicians generally use a moving average on the data to smooth out the daily swings. Investopedia.com

Interpretation

When the daily number is higher than the 10 day average than the market should be moving in a upwards direction and if the number is lower than the 10 day average the market should be moving lower, by combining the NYSE and the Nasdaq we can get a good feel of the direction of the market in general. I receive the new 52 week highs and the new 52 week lows from the investor's business daily (IBD) every day and made my own version of the formula using this information, with a 10 day average to smooth the findings

Example

On the next page there is an example of my 52 week high and 52 week low formula. The green colored areas are when the indexes are at their high, for the trend, and the red areas, are when the indexes are at the low of the trend. The last three columns are the indexes we are tracking with this formula. The triggers are the up and down columns. The 10day for the NYSE and the 10day for the NASDAQ and the 10 day for the NYSE and the NASDAQ working together to form a trigger. On 12/30/15 the indexes hit a high, the next day all the triggers are showing a down turn in the market. On 1/20/16 the indexes hit the low of the trend and on 2/1/16 it hit a high of the trend and the formula turned with in a day of the high and low of the move. On 2/11/16 the market hit a low of the trend and formula either gave us a signal that day or within two days of turning into an uptrend. This formula will help you stay on the correct side of the market trend, even if the trends are moving faster than normal as you can see in this example Never use one formula to make a buy or sell discussion. We never use one indicator or one formula to invest or track the market always use multiple indicators and formulas to Ensure a major trend and eliminate investing in a minor trend.

Tech Smart

Date	high	low	az/ba	10 day average	up	down	nasdac	high	low	aw/ax	10 day average	up	down	as/ay	at/az	up	down	Dow	S&P	Nasdaq
12/30/2015	39	23	1.70	1.17			5065.85	54	32	1.69	1.24			1.00	0.95	1		17603.87	2063.36	5065.85
12/31/2015	13	39	0.33	1.19		down	5007.41	3	45	0.71	1.28		1	0.47	0.93		down	17425.03	2043.94	5007.41
1/4/2016	4	135	0.03	1.15		1	4903.09	9	99	0.09	1.21		1	0.33	0.96		1	17148.94	2012.66	4903.09
1/5/2016	17	88	0.19	1.15		1	4891.43	18	59	0.31	1.17		1	0.63	0.98		1	17158.66	2016.71	4891.43
1/6/2015	36	257	0.14	1.15		1	4835.77	24	134	0.18	1.16		1	0.78	0.99		1	16906.51	1990.26	4835.77
1/7/2016	19	469	0.04	1.14		1	4689.43	24	134	0.18	1.13		1	0.23	1.01		1	16514.1	1943.09	4689.43
1/8/2016	11	503	0.02	1.11		1	4643.63	13	301	0.04	1.09		1	0.51	1.02		1	16346.45	1922.03	4643.63
1/11/2016	9	573	0.02	1.11		1	4637.99	11	395	0.03	0.96		1	0.56	0.77		1	16398.57	1923.67	4637.99
1/12/2016	7	545	0.01	0.74		1	4685.92	10	285	0.04	0.70		1	0.37	0.96		1	16516.22	1938.68	4685.92
1/13/2016	6	698	0.01	0.68		1	4526.06	10	443	0.02	0.59		1	0.38	0.90		1	16151.41	1890.28	4526.06
1/14/2016	5	657	0.01	0.53		1	4615	6	421	0.01	0.33		1	0.53	0.76		1	16379.05	1921.84	4615
1/15/2016	6	855	0.01	0.25		1	4488.42	4	518	0.01	0.16		1	0.91	0.50		1	15988.08	1880.33	4488.42
1/19/2016	9	629	0.01	0.08		1	4476.95	6	357	0.01	0.09		1	1.02	0.53		1	16016.02	1881.33	4476.95
1/20/2016	2	1218	0.00	0.05		1	4471.69	3	703	0.00	0.02		1	0.38	0.56		1	15766.74	1859.33	4471.69
1/21/2016	3	76	0.04	0.03	up		4472.06	3	80	0.04	0.06	1		1.05	0.55	1		15882.68	1868.99	4472.06
1/22/2016	10	21	0.48	0.06	1		4591.18	14	42	0.33	0.07	1		1.43	0.90	1		16093.51	1906.9	4591.18
1/21/2016	14	86	0.16	0.08	1		4518.49	9	80	0.11	0.07	1		1.45	1.18	1		15885.22	1877.08	4518.49
1/26/2016	17	65	0.26	0.10	1		4503.52	6	58	0.10	0.07	1		2.53	1.41	1		16167.23	1903.63	4503.52
1/27/2016	21	47	0.45	0.14	1		4468.17	9	72	0.13	0.08	1		3.57	1.78	1		15944.46	1882.95	4468.17
1/28/2016	26	100	0.26	0.17	1		4506.68	14	149	0.09	0.09	1		2.77	1.94	1		16069.64	1893.36	4506.68
1/29/2016	52	41	1.27	0.29	1		4613.95	30	82	0.37	0.12	1		3.47	2.43	1		16466.3	1940.24	4613.95
2/1/2016	68	34	2.00	0.49	1		4620.37	21	72	0.29	0.15	1		6.86	3.32	1		16449.18	1939.38	4620.37
2/2/2016	48	116	0.41	0.53		down	4516.95	20	111	0.18	0.17		1	2.30	3.22		1	16153.54	1903.03	4516.95
2/3/2016	71	212	0.33	0.57	1		4504.24	21	202	0.10	0.18	1		3.22	3.23		down	16336.66	1912.53	4504.24
2/4/2016	42	58	0.72	0.64	up		4509.56	10	66	0.15	0.19		1	4.78	3.36	1		16416.58	1915.45	4509.56
2/5/2016	50	141	0.35	0.67		down	4363.14	7	165	0.04	0.19		1	8.36	3.52		up	16204.97	1880.05	4363.14
2/8/2016	45	376	0.12	0.63		1	4283.75	8	439	0.02	0.16		1	6.57	3.99		1	16027.05	1853.44	4283.75
2/9/2016	55	370	0.15	0.63		1	4268.76	6	377	0.02	0.15		1	9.34	4.24		1	16014.38	1852.21	4268.76
2/10/2016	39	145	0.27	0.63		1	4283.59	6	163	0.04	0.14		1	6.26	4.43		1	15914.74	1851.86	4283.59
2/11/2016	33	535	0.06	0.60		1	4266.84	7	411	0.02	0.13		1	3.62	4.50		down	15660.18	1829.08	4266.84
2/12/2016	22	107	0.21	0.59		1	4337.51	9	105	0.09	0.13		1	2.40	4.49		1	15973.84	1864.78	4337.51
2/16/2016	18	46	0.39	0.50		1	4435.96	17	42	0.40	0.14	1		0.97	3.71		1	16196.41	1895.58	4435.96
2/17/2016	21	20	1.05	0.41	1		4926.82	19	32	0.59	0.17	1		1.77	2.46		1	16453.83	1926.82	4926.82

Moving Average Convergence/Divergence

MACD

Formula

12day=(Close x 15% + 85% of yesterday's ema 12day)26 day=(close x 7.5%+92.5% of yesterday's ema 26 day) (12 day minus 26 day) = moving average convergence / divergence, 9 day moving average of the (macd) is the signal, when the MACD crosses the 9day average of the MACD, that is the trigger. Note the formula has to be calculated for 26 days before the formula is effective.

Overview

Gerald Appel developed the MACD indicator in an attempt to chart momentum by measuring the increasing and decreasing space between two exponential moving averages. The MACD is calculated by subtracting the 26 day exponential moving average (EMA) from the 12-day EMA. A nine-day EMA of the MACD, called the "signal line", the signal is then plotted on top of the MACD, functioning as a trigger for buying and selling. We added a convergence and divergence column to the 9 day to see the movement of the 9 day and macd more easily, see chart on the next page.

Interpretation

To confirm changes in momentum, a nine-day exponential moving average is added as a signal line. A buy signal occurs when the MACD line crosses above the 9 day moving average. The sell signal occurs when the MACD line falls below the 9 day moving average. The MACD is a good formula to keep you on the right side of the market or issue. The macd signal will not give the high or low of the market or issue, the macd will usually turn when the move is approximately 20% completed ether high or low. Another signal to watch is when the MACD crosses above or below zero (center line) zero is considered the center line. When the MACD crosses above zero this is considered a bullish signal, and when the macd crosses below zero this is considered a bearish signal.

Example

On the chart on the next page there is an example of the MACD from 5/6/2015 to 6/9/2015. The red lines across the page, is when the DOW hit a low point in the trend and the green line is when the DOW hit a high of the trend. The last column is the convergence and divergence of the MACD, again the green areas, are when the MACD is showing a bullish signal and the red areas are when the MACD is showing a bearish trend. We also like to track the 12 day and 26 day EMA movement above and below the close of the market, we watch this as more of a confirmation or anticipation of the upcoming trend. When the 12 & 26 day EMA cross below the market the index should turn up and when the 12 & 26 day EMA turns above the market the index should turn down. Looking at the chart on the next page the DOW hit the low of the trend on 5/6/15 and the MACD turned up on 5/11/15 three days after the low and continued up untill 5/22/15. Another key indicator is the MACD moving above and below zero, above zero, is bullish and below zero is bearish. On 6/4/15 the MACD turned below zero (center line) and continued down to the low on 6/9/15. We never use one indicator or one formula to invest or track the market always use multiple indicators and formulas to ensure a major trend and eliminate investing in a minor trend.

Date	close	15%	85%	12 DAY	7.50%	92.50%	26 DAY	MACD	9 DAY	MACD 9 Day Convergence / Divergence
5/6/2015	17841.98	2676.30	15295.52	17971.82	1338.15	16627.85	17966.00	5.82	26.28	-20.46
5/7/2015	17924.06	2688.61	15276.05	17964.66	1344.30	16618.55	17962.85	1.80	22.96	-21.16
5/8/2015	18191.11	2728.67	15269.96	17998.62	1364.33	16615.64	17979.97	18.65	21.38	-2.73
5/11/2015	18105.17	2715.78	15298.83	18014.61	1357.89	16631.48	17989.36	25.24	19.85	5.39
5/12/2015	18068.23	2710.23	15312.41	18022.65	1355.12	16640.16	17995.28	27.37	18.71	8.66
5/13/2015	18060.49	2709.07	15319.25	18028.33	1354.54	16645.63	18000.17	28.16	19.43	8.73
5/14/2015	18252.24	2737.84	15324.08	18061.91	1368.92	16650.16	18019.07	42.84	21.68	21.16
5/15/2015	18215.07	2732.26	15352.63	18084.89	1366.13	16667.64	18033.77	51.11	24.41	26.70
5/18/2015	18298.88	2744.83	15372.15	18116.99	1372.42	16681.24	18053.66	63.33	29.37	33.96
5/19/2015	18312.39	2746.86	15399.44	18146.30	1373.43	16699.63	18073.06	73.23	36.86	36.37
5/20/2015	18285.4	2742.81	15424.35	18167.16	1371.41	16717.58	18088.99	78.17	45.35	32.83
5/21/2015	18285.74	2742.86	15442.09	18184.95	1371.43	16732.31	18103.74	81.20	52.30	28.91
5/22/2015	18232.02	2734.80	15457.21	18192.01	1367.40	16745.96	18113.36	78.64	58.23	20.42
5/26/2015	18041.54	2706.23	15463.21	18169.44	1353.12	16754.86	18107.98	61.46	62.02	(0.56)
5/27/2015	18162.99	2724.45	15444.02	18168.47	1362.22	16749.88	18112.10	56.37	65.15	(8.78)
5/28/2015	18126.12	2718.92	15443.2	18162.12	1359.46	16753.7	18113.15	48.96	65.83	(16.87)
5/29/2015	18010.68	2701.60	15437.8	18139.40	1350.80	16754.67	18105.47	33.93	63.92	(29.99)
6/1/2015	18040.37	2706.06	15418.49	18124.55	1353.03	16747.56	18100.59	23.96	59.55	(35.59)
6/2/2015	18011.94	2701.79	15405.87	18107.66	1350.90	16743.04	18093.94	13.72	52.94	(39.22)
6/3/2015	18076.27	2711.44	15391.51	18102.95	1355.72	16736.89	18092.61	10.34	45.40	(35.06)
6/4/2015	17905.58	2685.84	15387.51	18073.34	1342.92	16735.67	18078.59	-5.24	35.79	(41.04)
6/5/2015	17849.46	2677.42	15362.34	18039.76	1338.71	16722.69	18061.40	-21.64	24.65	(46.29)
6/8/2015	17766.55	2664.98	15333.8	17998.78	1332.49	16706.8	18039.29	-40.51	13.32	(53.83)
6/9/2015	17764.04	2664.61	15298.96	17963.57	1332.30	16686.34	18018.64	-55.08	0.94	(56.01)

Money Flow

Formula

The Money flow index is defined by dividing the moving average of the Accumulation/Distribution of an index or issue, by the moving average of the volume, I like to use a 14 day moving average.

Overview

Money flow is an indicator that provides insight on the amount of money flowing into the market or issue. When tracking the money flow index a tracking channel can be set up to indicate a bullish and bearish signal, below 20 and above 80 are the two levels, the money flow index travels between 80 high and 20 low, in most cases.

Interpretation

When money is flowing into an index or issue the price of the index or issue will move in an upwards direction, and as money flows out of the index or issue the price will move in a downwards direction. A good indicator, of the money flow index is when the index hits a high 80, or a low 20, 20 to buy and 80 to sell the issue. When the money flow index hits 80 or above this is an indicator that extreme amounts of money are flowing into the issue, this is usually a signal that the market is overbought and could turn bearish, and when the index hits 20 or below, it is oversold and could turn bullish, one note to remember the index or issue could stay over bought or over sold for an extended amount of time that is why we use more than one indicator for our trigger to buy or sell.

Example

On the chart on the next page you can see an example of the money flow index and the NASDAQ. We track the money flow index by using stock charts .com. We track the daily flow up or down and as an overbought or oversold indicator, when the index hits highs of 80 and lows of 20. On 11/13/15 the NASDAQ hit a low for the trend, and the money flow index is showing a downwards trend. On 11/16/15 the money flow index turns up as the market move in a bullish direction. On 12/1/15 the money flow starts to fade, the market hits its high on 12/1/15 and on the next day the market turns down as does the money flow index. The money flow index is a good indicator, but no one indicator should be used as a trigger, always use multiple indicators and information before investing.

Money Flow Index

Date	Nasdaq	MFI	Up	Down
11/13/2015	4,927.98			1
11/16/2015	4,984.62		1	
11/17/2015	4,986.02		1	
11/18/2015	5,075.20		1	
11/19/2015	5,073.64		1	
11/20/2015	5,104.92		1	
11/23/2015	5,102.48			1
11/24/2015	5,102.81			1
11/25/2015	5,116.14		1	
11/27/2015	5,127.52			1
11/30/2015	5,108.67			1
12/1/2015	5,156.31		1	
12/2/2015	5,123.22			1
12/3/2015	5,037.53			1
12/4/2015	5,142.27		1	
12/7/2015	5,101.81			1
12/8/2015	5,098.24			1
12/9/2015	5,022.87			1
12/10/2015	5,045.17			1
12/11/2015	4,933.48			1
12/14/2015	4,952.23			1
12/15/2015	4,995.36		1	
12/16/2015	5,071.13		1	
12/17/2015	5,002.55			1
12/18/2015	4,923.08			1

Moving Averages

Formula

The moving average of a stock or issue, for each period is calculated as the average price over the last n-periods. This is done everyday, so each day yields a slightly different number showing the average movement for the period when viewed over time.

Overview

Moving average is an indicator that displays the average value of a security price over a period of time. A moving average compares the correlation between a moving average of the security price with the security itself. There are several different types of moving averages, simple, arithmetic, Exponential, time series, triangular, variable, volume, adjusted, and weighted. It is also common to do a moving average of another moving average of various time frames. When the price crosses above the moving average it may be a good time to buy, and when the price crosses below the moving average it may be a good time to sell

Interpretation

When using moving averages, we like to use several different averages in conjunction with each other to form a buy and sell signal. For example, witch you can see on the next page we generate several moving averages from a five day to two hundred day moving average. A five day average is used as a short term indicator and the two hundred day is use as a long term indicator. We also use different moving averages in conjunction with each other to form an indicator. For a short term indicator, we use the five day, nine day, and twenty day moving average. For a mid-range indicator, we use the five day and the twenty day, the nine day and the twenty day, and the twenty day and the fifty day. The long term indicator is the fifty day and the one hundred day, and the one hundred day and the two hundred day.

Example

On the chart on the next page, the green area across the page is the high of the trend and the red areas are the low of the trend. Under the moving average section, the green is the buy signal and the red is the sell signal. The trigger is when we see two shaded areas turn green (up) or red (down) that is the buy and sell trigger. On 12/12/13 the Dow Jones close at 15739.43 for a low of the trend. The moving average turned, positive (up) for, both the five and nine day on 12/16/13. The Dow Jones move up as did the moving averages until we hit the high on 12/31/13, The five day turned the next day and confirmation hit (nine day) on 1/6/14. On 1/15/14 and 1/17/14 you can see a minor up trend and then the Dow Jones dropped another thousand points before hitting the low of the trend on 2/3/14. Knowing the main trend secondary trend and a minor trend is key and therefore we never invest just using one formula always use multiple formulas before you invest it will increase your chance of making a good trade either up or down. On 2/3/14 the Dow Jones five day moving average was a negative 344.72 and the nine day was a negative 502.23, any time an index or stock has a major upswing or a major down swing the moving average will lag behind some of the other indicator, but the moving averages will help to keep you on the right side of the trend. We never use one indicator or one formula to invest or track the market always use multiple indicators and formulas to insure a major trend and eliminate investing in a minor trend.

Tech Smart

Date	close	5.00	9.00	20.00	50.00	100	200	close/5	close/9	close/20	5/20	9/20	20/50	50/100	100/200
12/12/2013	15,739.43	15,920.37	15,915.17	15,966.11	15,639.64	15,452.18	15,181.49	(180.94)	(175.74)	(226.68)	(45.74)	(50.94)	275.53	187.46	270.69
12/13/2013	15,755.36	15,867.40	15,887.01	15,960.07	15,654.82	15,454.31	15,189.82	(112.04)	(131.65)	(204.70)	(92.66)	(73.05)	232.20	200.51	264.49
12/16/2013	15,884.57	15,839.21	15,883.67	15,956.21	15,671.06	15,457.60	15,198.60	45.36	0.90	(71.64)	(117.00)	(72.53)	212.62	213.46	259.00
12/17/2013	15,875.26	15,819.63	15,882.06	15,951.17	15,689.84	15,460.76	15,206.71	55.63	(6.80)	(75.91)	(131.54)	(69.11)	192.22	214.07	254.05
12/18/2013	16,167.97	15,884.52	15,920.56	15,961.22	15,717.67	15,467.22	15,216.29	283.45	247.41	206.75	(76.70)	(40.65)	202.89	250.44	250.94
12/19/2013	16,179.08	15,972.45	15,938.21	15,975.13	15,745.19	15,473.81	15,225.54	206.63	240.87	203.95	(2.68)	36.92	193.02	271.38	248.27
12/20/2013	16,221.14	16,065.60	15,959.95	15,985.69	15,767.09	15,481.03	15,234.66	155.54	261.19	235.45	79.92	(25.74)	192.86	286.06	246.37
12/23/2013	16,294.61	16,147.61	15,995.66	15,997.18	15,788.24	15,487.70	15,243.89	147.00	298.95	297.43	150.43	(1.52)	207.42	300.54	243.80
12/24/2013	16,357.55	16,244.07	16,052.77	16,011.43	15,809.37	15,494.69	15,253.43	113.48	304.78	346.12	232.64	41.34	243.41	314.68	241.26
12/26/2013	16,479.88	16,306.45	16,135.05	16,031.78	15,835.60	15,503.37	15,263.55	173.43	344.83	448.10	274.67	103.26	299.44	332.24	239.81
12/27/2013	16,478.41	16,366.32	16,215.39	16,050.84	15,857.69	15,512.96	15,273.25	112.09	263.02	427.57	315.48	164.55	357.69	344.73	239.71
12/30/2013	16,504.35	16,422.96	16,284.25	16,071.74	15,880.35	15,523.30	15,283.20	81.39	220.10	432.61	351.22	212.51	403.90	357.05	240.10
12/31/2013	16,576.66	16,479.37	16,362.18	16,100.13	15,903.89	15,534.08	15,293.82	97.29	214.48	476.53	379.24	262.05	458.29	369.81	240.26
1/2/2014	16,441.35	16,496.13	16,392.56	16,126.47	15,924.87	15,544.24	15,303.75	(54.78)	48.79	314.88	369.66	266.09	467.69	380.63	240.49
1/3/2014	16,469.99	16,494.15	16,424.88	16,155.48	15,944.92	15,554.74	15,313.56	(24.16)	45.11	314.51	338.67	269.40	479.96	390.18	241.20
1/6/2014	16,425.10	16,483.49	16,447.54	16,188.66	15,965.15	15,564.48	15,323.56	(58.39)	(22.44)	239.44	297.83	261.89	482.40	400.66	240.92
1/7/2014	16,530.94	16,488.81	16,473.80	16,211.19	15,985.58	15,576.42	15,333.66	42.13	57.14	319.75	277.61	262.61	488.22	409.17	242.76
1/8/2014	16,462.74	16,466.02	16,485.49	16,233.05	16,003.42	15,589.92	15,343.73	(3.28)	(22.75)	229.69	232.97	252.44	482.07	413.50	246.19
1/9/2014	16,444.36	16,466.63	16,481.54	16,256.61	16,020.93	15,603.55	15,353.15	(22.27)	(37.18)	187.75	210.01	224.93	460.61	417.38	250.40
1/10/2014	16,437.05	16,460.04	16,476.95	16,286.29	16,036.06	15,617.81	15,362.71	(22.99)	(39.90)	150.76	173.75	190.66	440.88	418.25	255.11
1/13/2014	16,257.94	16,426.61	16,449.57	16,312.22	16,048.85	15,630.36	15,371.10	(168.67)	(191.63)	(54.28)	114.39	137.35	400.77	418.48	259.26
1/14/2014	16,373.86	16,395.19	16,427.04	16,343.14	16,065.43	15,645.13	15,380.11	(21.33)	(53.18)	30.72	52.05	83.90	361.61	400.30	265.02
1/15/2014	16,481.94	16,399.03	16,431.55	16,373.01	16,082.75	15,660.31	15,389.21	82.91	50.39	108.93	26.02	58.54	348.79	422.44	271.10
1/16/2014	16,417.01	16,393.56	16,425.66	16,400.10	16,098.31	15,674.37	15,398.54	23.45	(8.65)	16.91	(6.54)	25.56	327.35	423.94	275.83
1/17/2014	16,458.56	16,397.86	16,429.38	16,414.63	16,115.12	15,689.50	15,407.81	60.70	29.18	43.93	(16.76)	14.75	314.26	425.62	281.69
1/21/2014	16,414.44	16,429.16	16,416.43	16,426.39	16,128.47	15,705.88	15,417.05	(14.72)	(1.99)	(11.95)	2.77	(9.96)	287.96	422.59	288.83
1/22/2014	16,373.34	16,429.06	16,406.50	16,434.00	16,144.06	15,721.37	15,425.85	(55.72)	(33.16)	(60.66)	(4.95)	(27.50)	262.44	422.69	295.52
1/23/2014	16,197.35	16,372.14	16,379.05	16,429.14	16,152.77	15,734.93	15,433.47	(174.79)	(181.70)	(231.79)	(57.00)	(50.09)	226.29	417.84	301.46
1/24/2014	15,879.11	16,264.56	16,317.06	16,405.22	16,154.69	15,745.62	15,438.85	(385.45)	(437.95)	(526.11)	(140.66)	(88.16)	162.37	409.07	306.76
1/27/2014	15,837.88	16,140.42	16,270.39	16,373.12	16,156.43	15,755.66	15,443.72	(302.54)	(432.51)	(535.24)	(232.69)	(102.73)	113.96	400.77	311.94
1/28/2014	15,928.56	16,043.25	16,220.91	16,345.63	16,158.57	15,765.63	15,449.04	(114.69)	(292.35)	(417.07)	(302.38)	(124.72)	62.34	392.94	316.60
1/29/2014	15,738.79	15,916.34	16,138.34	16,307.35	16,155.82	15,773.65	15,454.73	(177.55)	(399.55)	(568.56)	(391.01)	(169.01)	(17.48)	382.17	318.91
1/30/2014	15,848.61	15,846.59	16,075.18	16,270.95	16,153.56	15,782.72	15,460.19	2.02	(226.57)	(422.34)	(424.36)	(195.76)	(78.38)	370.84	322.53
1/31/2014	15,698.85	15,810.54	15,990.77	16,233.82	16,148.02	15,789.08	15,465.59	(111.69)	(291.92)	(534.97)	(423.28)	(243.05)	(157.25)	358.94	323.48
2/3/2014	15,372.80	15,717.52	15,875.03	16,178.96	16,136.13	15,790.89	15,469.77	(344.72)	(502.23)	(806.16)	(461.44)	(303.93)	(261.10)	345.24	321.12
2/4/2014	15,445.24	15,620.86	15,771.91	16,129.97	16,127.02	15,792.08	15,474.26	(175.62)	(326.67)	(684.73)	(509.11)	(358.06)	(355.11)	334.94	317.82
2/5/2014	15,440.23	15,561.15	15,687.79	16,075.43	16,115.63	15,793.48	15,478.63	(120.92)	(247.56)	(635.20)	(514.29)	(387.65)	(427.84)	322.15	314.85
2/6/2014	15,628.53	15,517.13	15,659.94	16,033.72	16,106.90	15,796.00	15,483.17	111.40	(31.41)	(405.19)	(516.59)	(373.78)	(446.96)	310.90	312.83
2/7/2014	15,794.08	15,536.18	15,655.08	16,001.01	16,101.33	15,799.00	15,488.76	257.90	139.00	(207.13)	(465.03)	(346.13)	(446.25)	302.33	310.24
2/10/2014	15,801.79	15,621.97	15,640.99	15,969.45	16,095.91	15,801.72	15,494.27	179.82	160.80	(167.66)	(347.47)	(328.45)	(454.92)	294.19	307.45
2/11/2014	15,994.77	15,731.88	15,669.43	15,956.29	16,093.86	15,804.90	15,500.68	262.89	325.34	38.48	(224.41)	(286.85)	(424.43)	298.96	304.22
2/12/2014	15,963.94	15,836.62	15,682.25	15,935.79	16,091.41	15,808.17	15,506.00	127.32	281.69	28.15	(99.17)	(253.54)	(409.16)	283.24	301.77
2/13/2014	16,027.59	15,916.43	15,718.77	15,913.07	16,091.79	15,813.93	15,512.34	111.16	308.82	114.52	3.36	(194.30)	(373.01)	277.85	301.59
2/14/2014	16,154.39	15,988.50	15,805.62	15,899.94	16,096.58	15,821.46	15,519.61	165.89	348.77	254.45	88.55	(94.32)	(290.96)	275.12	301.86
2/18/2014	16,130.40	16,054.22	15,881.75	15,883.53	16,101.39	15,829.42	15,526.10	76.18	248.65	246.87	170.68	(1.79)	(219.65)	271.97	303.32

49

OPEN 10 TRIN TRADING INDEX

Formula

(10 periods total of advancing issues / 10 periods of declining issues)

(10 periods of total advancing volume / 10 periods of total declining volume)

MOVING AVERAGES

Overview

The open 10 TRIN is a smoothed variation of the arms index. It is a market breadth indicator that uses advancing/ declining volume and advancing/declining issues to measure the strength of the market.

Interpretation

The open 10 TRIN is like the arms index but with a 10 day moving average. In general, when the open 10 TRIN is moving up to 1.0 the market condition is considered bearish, and when the value of the open 10 TRIN is moving down to .80 the market condition is bullish

Example

On the next page we have an example of the NASDAQ from 9/16/16 to 11/7/16 using both the arms index and the open 10 TRIN. Looking at the chart on the next page you can see the difference in volatility between the arms index, and the open 10 TRIN. The open 10 TRIN has three different ranges that are being tracked, the 4 day the 10 day. And the 21 day. The 4 day is a more volatile indicator that is good for a short term indicator. The 10 day is a more stable indicator that will help you stay on the right side of the market in most cases. The 21 day indicator is for a longer term indicator. We like to track all three time frames and use them in conjunction with each other to form a more smoothed scenario of the market. Referring to the chart we can see the arms index at work, in conjunction with the open 10 TRIN. The open 10 TRIN provides a down signal in the 10 day column on 10/17/16 along with the arms index. This provides a signal that the uptrend may reverse, as it did on 11/4/16 to 5046.37, for a total of 153.45 points. We never use one indicator or one formula to invest or track the market always use multiple indicators and formulas to ensure a major trend and eliminate investing in a minor trend.

A	B	C	D	E	F	G	H
nasdac	close	advancing	declining	advancing	declining	arms index	
9/16/2016	5244.57	1310	1550	1,147,075,887.00	1,843,802,534.00	0.85	0.62
9/19/2016	5235.03	1691	1168	1,040,478,862.00	715,733,695.00	1.45	1.45
9/20/2016	5241.35	1351	1481	797,086,777.00	880,572,573.00	0.91	0.91
9/21/2016	5295.18	2061	777	1,554,877,897.00	429,782,335.00	2.65	3.62
9/22/2016	5339.52	2040	806	1,495,986,385.00	380,375,401.00	2.53	3.93
9/23/2016	5305.75	1056	1763	653,844,150.00	1,086,671,926.00	0.60	0.60
9/26/2016	5257.49	689	2178	511,863,903.00	1,137,761,023.00	0.32	0.45
9/27/2016	5305.71	1876	975	1,244,541,778.00	490,509,225.00	1.92	2.54
9/28/2016	5318.55	1699	1142	1,029,380,948.00	723,748,667.00	1.49	1.42
9/29/2016	5269.15	698	2166	1,945,892,474.00	601,846,781.00	0.32	3.23
9/30/2016	5312.00	2074	773	1,551,226,365.00	488,685,030.00	2.68	3.17
10/3/2016	5300.87	1181	1656	777,822,017.00	803,648,499.00	0.71	0.97
10/4/2016	5289.66	1076	1746	654,432,952.00	1,036,772,343.00	0.62	0.63
10/5/2016	5316.02	1941	889	1,120,968,534.00	606,426,425.00	2.18	1.85
10/6/2016	5306.85	1108	1704	712,927,743.00	901,723,762.00	0.65	0.79
10/7/2016	5292.40	968	1820	574,252,863.00	992,036,607.00	0.53	0.58
10/10/2016	5328.67	1984	842	871,179,021.00	471,098,593.00	2.36	1.85
10/11/2016	5246.79	468	2392	252,957,885.00	1,534,675,173.00	0.20	0.16
10/12/2016	5239.02	1327	1450	637,740,145.00	902,224,696.00	0.92	0.71
10/13/2016	5213.80	794	2030	548,958,508.00	1,113,855,871.00	0.39	0.49
10/14/2016	5214.16	1352	1440	825,297,544.00	737,794,367.00	0.94	1.12
10/17/2016	5199.82	1142	1683	483,355,999.00	868,407,965.00	0.68	0.56
10/18/2016	5243.84	1806	999	1,070,024,687.00	392,508,729.00	1.81	2.73
10/19/2016	5246.41	1660	1092	889,350,664.00	630,568,709.00	1.52	1.41
10/20/2016	5241.83	1287	1491	795,675,822.00	917,041,622.00	0.86	0.87
10/21/2016	5257.40	1251	1505	807,499,522.00	817,001,045.00	0.83	0.99
10/24/2016	5309.83	1680	1121	1,042,132,090.00	446,058,638.00	1.50	2.34
10/25/2016	5283.40	876	1907	575,233,683.00	987,515,835.00	0.46	0.58
10/26/2016	5250.27	863	1923	675,577,500.00	1,022,273,714.00	0.45	0.66
10/27/2016	5215.97	917	1858	549,480,939.00	1,343,914,146.00	0.49	0.41
10/28/2016	5190.10	1138	1623	711,539,954.00	1,097,111,201.00	0.70	0.65
10/31/2016	5189.13	1391	1428	855,697,628.00	822,459,463.00	0.97	1.04
11/1/2016	5153.58	848	1942	515,863,101.00	1,334,633,871.00	0.44	0.39
11/2/2016	5105.37	726	2071	614,509,994.00	1,484,103,533.00	0.35	0.41
11/3/2016	5058.41	954	1844	593,107,919.00	1,454,334,123.00	0.52	0.41
11/4/2016	5046.37	1437	1329	945,658,619.00	1,050,073,997.00	1.08	0.90
11/7/2016	5166.17	2269	564	1,617,396,584.00	272,102,612.00	4.02	5.94

I	J	K	L	M	N	O	P	Q	R
	UP	DOWN	4 day sum	4 day sum	4 day sum	4 day sum	g/h	i/j	70/1.25k/l
1.36		1	6676	7518	5,484,286,166.00	5,189,158,353.00	0.89	1.06	0.84
1.00	1		6312	7903	4,803,850,792.00	5,639,090,448.00	0.80	0.85	0.94
1.01		1	7128	7047	5,122,571,856.00	4,933,665,094.00	1.01	1.04	0.97
0.73	1		7801	6400	5,608,484,588.00	4,616,669,283.00	1.22	1.21	1.00
0.64	1		8453	5782	6,035,505,808.00	4,250,266,538.00	1.46	1.42	1.03
1.00	1		8199	5995	5,542,274,071.00	3,493,135,930.00	1.37	1.59	0.86
0.70	1		7197	7005	5,013,659,112.00	3,915,163,258.00	1.03	1.28	0.80
0.76	1		7722	6499	5,461,114,113.00	3,525,099,910.00	1.19	1.55	0.77
1.05		1	7360	6864	4,935,617,164.00	3,819,066,242.00	1.07	1.29	0.83
0.10	1		6018	8224	5,385,523,253.00	4,040,537,622.00	0.73	1.33	0.55
0.85	1		7036	7234	6,282,905,468.00	3,442,550,726.00	0.97	1.83	0.53
0.74	1		7528	6712	6,548,863,582.00	3,108,438,202.00	1.12	2.11	0.53
0.98	1		6728	7483	5,958,754,756.00	3,654,701,320.00	0.90	1.63	0.55
1.18		1	6970	7230	6,050,342,342.00	3,537,379,078.00	0.96	1.71	0.56
0.82	1		7380	6768	4,817,377,611.00	3,837,256,059.00	1.09	1.26	0.87
0.92	1		6274	7815	3,840,404,109.00	4,340,607,636.00	0.80	0.88	0.91
1.27		1	7077	7001	3,933,761,113.00	4,008,057,730.00	1.01	0.98	1.03
1.19		1	6469	7647	3,532,286,046.00	4,505,960,560.00	0.85	0.78	1.08
1.29		1	5855	8208	3,049,057,657.00	4,801,758,831.00	0.71	0.63	1.12
0.79	1		5541	8534	2,885,088,422.00	5,013,890,940.00	0.65	0.58	1.13
0.84	1		5925	8154	3,136,133,103.00	4,759,648,700.00	0.73	0.66	1.10
1.22		1	5083	8995	2,748,310,081.00	5,156,958,072.00	0.57	0.53	1.06
0.66	1		6421	7602	3,565,376,883.00	4,014,791,628.00	0.84	0.89	0.95
1.08		1	6754	7244	3,816,987,402.00	3,743,135,641.00	0.93	1.02	0.91
0.99	1		7247	6705	4,063,704,716.00	3,546,321,392.00	1.08	1.15	0.94
0.84	1		7146	6770	4,045,906,694.00	3,625,528,070.00	1.06	1.12	0.95
0.64	1		7684	6208	4,604,682,785.00	3,203,178,743.00	1.24	1.44	0.86
0.79	1		6754	7116	4,109,891,781.00	3,798,185,849.00	0.95	1.08	0.88
0.68	1		5957	7947	3,896,118,617.00	4,189,890,854.00	0.75	0.93	0.81
1.21		1	5587	8314	3,649,923,734.00	4,616,763,378.00	0.67	0.79	0.85
1.08		1	5474	8432	3,553,964,166.00	4,896,873,534.00	0.65	0.73	0.89
0.94	1		5185	8739	3,367,529,704.00	5,273,274,359.00	0.59	0.64	0.93
1.13		1	5157	8774	3,308,159,122.00	5,620,392,395.00	0.59	0.59	1.00
0.85	1		5020	8922	3,247,091,616.00	6,082,222,214.00	0.56	0.53	1.05
1.27		1	5057	8908	3,290,718,596.00	6,192,642,191.00	0.57	0.53	1.07
1.20		1	5356	8614	3,524,837,261.00	6,145,604,987.00	0.62	0.57	1.08
0.68	1		6234	7750	4,286,536,217.00	5,595,248,136.00	0.80	0.77	1.05

T	U	V	W	X	Y	Z
10 day sum c	10 day sum d	10 day sum e	10 day sum f	p/q	r/s	.80/1.00 t/u 10
15223	16104	10514660375	10817703264	0.95	0.97	0.97
15399	15953	10642496731	10881689234	0.97	0.98	0.99
14816	16577	10436486678	11311403297	0.89	0.92	0.97
15316	16003	10951518191	11021478903	0.96	0.99	0.96
15622	15669	11360914418	10627821003	1.00	1.07	0.93
15279	15996	11222250206	10689541978	0.96	1.05	0.91
15564	15691	11538424140	9820055306	0.99	1.17	0.84
15385	15883	11062051682	10044762931	0.97	1.10	0.88
16549	14688	11613066917	9182513671	1.13	1.26	0.89
15859	15430	12489994226	9037582306	1.03	1.38	0.74
16545	14779	12972255426	8779489190	1.12	1.48	0.76
16416	14885	12603001556	7739335155	1.10	1.63	0.68
15801	15463	12216955646	8060373803	1.02	1.52	0.67
16391	14871	12540837403	7786227655	1.10	1.61	0.68
15438	15798	11698887249	8258169082	0.98	1.42	0.69
14366	16812	10777153727	8869830288	0.85	1.22	0.70
15294	15891	10994488598	8254256955	0.96	1.33	0.72
15073	16105	10735582580	8651171105	0.94	1.24	0.75
14524	16580	10128780947	9062886576	0.88	1.12	0.78
13619	17468	9648358507	9452993780	0.78	1.02	0.76
14273	16742	8527763577	9588941366	0.85	0.89	0.96
13341	17652	7459893211	9968664301	0.76	0.75	1.01
13966	16995	7752095881	9557524531	0.82	0.81	1.01
14550	16341	7987013593	9151320897	0.89	0.87	1.02
13896	16943	7661720881	9461936094	0.82	0.81	1.01
14039	16744	7756292660	9377213377	0.84	0.83	1.01
14751	16045	8224171887	8831235408	0.92	0.93	0.99
13643	17110	7928226549	9347652650	0.80	0.85	0.94
14038	16641	8350846164	8835251191	0.84	0.95	0.89
13628	17049	8262586958	9276940641	0.80	0.89	0.90
13972	16642	8425168404	9260195971	0.84	0.91	0.92
14011	16630	8455568488	9344861067	0.84	0.90	0.93
13717	16889	8488075590	9811086973	0.81	0.87	0.94
12637	17961	8032560897	10902681777	0.70	0.74	0.95
11931	18713	7736318152	11726447191	0.64	0.66	0.97
12081	18551	7886300949	11859479566	0.65	0.66	0.98
13099	17610	8696198011	11314581133	0.74	0.77	0.97

	AB	AC	AD	AE	AF	AG	AH	AI	AJ	AK	AL
							.85/1.10	.75/1.25	.80/1.00		
	21 DAY C	21 DAY D	21 DAY E	21DAY F	ag/ah	ai/ad	21	4day	10 day	up	down
	31156	31322	19663524151	18893163315	0.99	1.04	0.96	0.84	0.97		1
	31692	30840	19858817573	18729962936	1.03	1.06	0.97	0.94	0.99		1
	31097	31438	19683712056	18947275940	0.99	1.04	0.95	0.97	0.97		1
	31819	30730	20331578373	18755227244	1.04	1.08	0.96	1.00	0.96		1
	32327	30245	20995183848	18430843981	1.07	1.14	0.94	1.03	0.93		1
	31541	31023	20573740876	19065473814	1.02	1.08	0.94	0.86	0.91		1
	31267	31311	20609892794	18981618796	1.00	1.09	0.92	0.80	0.84		1
	31663	30970	21089980552	18760886722	1.02	1.12	0.91	0.77	0.88		1
	32023	30610	21228145205	18829757090	1.05	1.13	0.93	0.83	0.89		1
	30930	31703	22277487974	18991224038	0.98	1.17	0.83	0.55	0.74	1	
	31504	31149	23056827092	18750507840	1.01	1.23	0.82	0.53	0.76	1	
	31639	30989	23117661931	18557038419	1.02	1.25	0.82	0.53	0.68	1	
	31200	31416	22859452377	18942063037	0.99	1.21	0.82	0.55	0.67	1	
	31207	31448	22977324081	19097630952	0.99	1.20	0.82	0.56	0.68	1	
	30754	31801	22650405440	19279647985	0.97	1.17	0.82	0.87	0.69	1	
	29988	32481	22138068145	19497651291	0.92	1.14	0.81	0.91	0.70	1	
	30573	31887	22216738804	18943798933	0.96	1.17	0.82	1.03	0.72	1	
	30637	31796	22274006720	18471226411	0.96	1.21	0.80	1.08	0.75	1	
	29909	32463	21190832629	19107649507	0.92	1.11	0.83	1.12	0.78	1	
	30168	32156	21261425424	18635507451	0.94	1.14	0.82	1.13	0.76	1	
	30132	32172	21017757803	18626523672	0.94	1.13	0.83	1.10	0.96	1	
	29886	32431	20432148637	18748153491	0.92	1.09	0.85	1.06	1.01	1	1
	30382	31880	20355097437	17296859686	0.95	1.18	0.81	0.95	1.01	1	1
	30351	31804	20203969239	17211694700	0.95	1.17	0.81	0.91	1.02	1	1
	30287	31814	20202558284	17248163749	0.95	1.17	0.81	0.94	1.01	1	1
	29477	32542	19455179909	17635382459	0.91	1.10	0.82	0.95	1.01	1	1
	29117	32857	19001325614	17701065696	0.89	1.07	0.83	0.86	0.99	1	
	28937	33001	18922715147	17601909605	0.88	1.08	0.82	0.88	0.94	1	
	29111	32746	19086428744	17486422296	0.89	1.09	0.81	0.81	0.89	1	
	28152	33629	18391367905	18339827217	0.84	1.00	0.83	0.85	0.90	1	
	27591	34110	18073526911	18713189751	0.81	0.97	0.84	0.89	0.92	1	
	28284	33372	16983332065	18933802433	0.85	0.90	0.94	0.93	0.93	1	
	27058	34541	15947968801	19779751274	0.78	0.81	0.97	1.00	0.94	1	
	26603	34956	15784656778	20460206308	0.76	0.77	0.99	1.05	0.95	1	
	26481	35054	15723331745	20877768088	0.76	0.75	1.00	1.07	0.97	1	
	25977	35494	15548021830	21321415660	0.73	0.73	1.00	1.08	0.98	1	
	27138	34354	16452490671	20691794510	0.79	0.80	0.99	1.05	0.97	1	

Parabolic SAR

Formula

P (T) =P (T-1) +AF X (EP (T-1)-P (T-1)

Where;

P (t) – current value of the indicator

P (t-1) – value in the previous period

Af- acceleration factor generally rising from 0.02 to 0.2 with a step of 0.02

Ep (t-1) – extreme price in the previous period

Overview

The parabolic SAR was developed by Welles Wilder it is a trend following indicator designed to confirm or deny a trend direction. It also determines a trend end, corrections or flat stages as well as exit points. The basic principle of the indicator can be described as "stop and reverse" (SAR).

Interpretation

The Parabolic SAR is a popular tool, but it has its limitations and in a changing market it can give false signals. For trend confirmation the indicator is plotted below the price for an uptrend and above the price for a down trend. The Parabolic SAR trails prices as the trend extends over time, in this regard the indicator stops and reverses when the price trend reverses and breaks above or below the indicator. The convergence / divergence between the current price and the Parabolic SAR provides the trend indicator. When the convergence / divergence continues to increase that signals continued upward movement. When the convergence / divergence continues to decrease this signal continued downward movement.

Example

The parabolic SAR chart on the next page is an example of the SAR at work. The Parabolic SAR is not the best indicator in a fast moving mark as you can see on the chart on the next page. Looking at the chart on the next page you can see the Parabolic SAR on the correct side of the S&P at the high and at the low of the trend, we added a convergence / divergence column to provide the strength of the Parabolic SAR. Looking at the chart the convergence / divergence weakens before the SAR changes to a downwards turn and strengthens before it turns to an upwards signal. Adding the convergence / divergence column provides us with a signal a few days prior to the Parabolic SAR signal.

DATE	CLOSE	parabolic sar	convergence/ divergence	up	down
4/18/2016	2094.34	2038.95	55.39	1	
4/19/2016	2100.8	2042.29	58.51	1	
4/20/2016	2102.4	2047.23	55.17	1	
4/21/2016	2091.48	2052	39.48	1	
4/22/2016	2091.58	2059.36	32.22	1	
4/25/2016	2087.79	2064.5	23.29	1	
4/26/2016	2091.7	2069.18	22.52	1	
4/27/2016	2095.15	2073.36	21.79	1	
4/28/2016	2075.81	2111.05	-35.24		1
4/29/2016	2065.3	2110.26	-44.96		1
5/3/2016	2081.43	2107.94	-26.51		1
5/4/2016	2063.37	2105.72	-42.35		1
5/5/2016	2050.63	2100.01	-49.38		1
5/6/2016	2057.14	2096.82	-39.68		1
5/9/2016	2058.69	2092.23	-33.54		1
5/10/2016	2084.99	2088.01	-3.02		1
5/11/2016	2064.46	2084.87	-20.41		1
5/12/2016	2064.11	2084.25	-20.14		1
5/13/2016	2046.61	2083.29	-36.68		1
5/16/2016	2066.66	2079.78	-13.12		1
5/17/2016	2047.21	2076.56	-29.35		1
5/18/2016	2047.63	2073.59	-25.96		1
5/19/2016	2040.04	2069.68	-29.64		1
5/20/2016	2052.32	2064.43	-12.11		1
5/23/2016	2048.04	2059.8	-11.76		1
5/24/2016	2076.06	2051.91	24.15	1	
5/26/2016	2090.1	2029.7	60.4	1	
5/27/2016	2099.06	2032.3	66.76	1	
5/31/2016	2096.96	2036.7	60.26	1	
6/1/2016	2099.33	2041	58.33	1	
6/2/2016	2105.26	2046.62	58.64	1	
6/3/2016	2099.13	2052.48	46.65	1	
6/6/2014	2109	2057.76	51.24	1	
6/7/2016	2112.13	2064.43	47.7	1	
6/8/2016	2119.12	2072.1	47.02	1	
6/9/2016	2115.48	2080.65	34.83	1	
6/10/2016	2096.07	2086.37	9.7	1	
6/13/2016	2079.06	2120.55	-41.49		1

Pivot Point with Fibonacci Points

Pivot Points

Formula

Pivot point p = (high + low + close) /3
Support 1 s1 = (p x 2) −high
Support 2 s2 = p − (high − low)
Resistance 1 r1 = (p x 2) − low
Resistance 2 r2 = p + (high − low)

Overview

Pivot Points were originally used by traders to set crucial levels of convergence and divergence.

The pivot point would be set up by using the high and low from the day before, once the formula is set in place the levels are set for the day. Pivot points can be used to determine support and resistance levels and directional movement.

Interpretation

Pivot points are support or resistance levels. Pivot Points have five indicators, (p) is the middle of the line. When the issue moves above the pivot point (p) the move is considered bullish, when it move above the first resistance level, it shows the issue has even move strength. When the issue moves below the Pivot point (p) the move is considered bearish or weak. When the issue breaks below the support level (s1) this means the issue has even more weakness, with the next target (s2).

Example

Pivot points can be set up for several different scenarios and time frames. The 1,5,10, and 15 minute charts are set up by using the high low and close from the day before. The 30 and 60 minute charts are set up by using the week prior's data, at the end of the week the data is calculated, by using the high low and close of the week before. The new data last for the entire week. For the daily chart we would use April's data for the month of May. The high low and close for April would remain fixed for the month of May and then on June 1 we would use the May data high low and close for June pivot points, and the data would last for the month of June. The pivot points we use in this formula, are set by using the numbers from the month before to receive our daily data. We also like to use the pivot points in conjunction with the Fibonacci numbers, as you can see on the next page some of the pivot points and the Fibonacci points are in range of each other. The scenario on the next page the Dow jones fell below the pivot points and between the 2.618 and the 4.236 Fibonacci to 15882.68 on 1/21/16. We never use one indicator or one formula to invest or track the market always use multiple indicators and formulas to insure a major trend and eliminate investing in a minor trend.

Date	Dow Jones	Fibonacci	Numbers	Trigger
12/29/2015	17720.98	0.236	139.81	17581.17
12/18/2015	17128.55	0.382	226.31	17494.67
move	592.43	0.5	296.22	17424.77
		0.618	366.12	17354.86
r2	18265.96	1	592.43	17128.55
r1	17845.5	1.618	958.55	16762.43
p	17481.11	2.618	1550.98	16170.00
s1	17060.65	4.236	2509.53	15211.45
s2	16696.26			

Dow Jones

DATE	CLOSE	POSITIVE	NEGATIVE
12/18/2015	17128.55	0.00	367.29
12/21/2015	17251.62	123.07	0.00
12/22/2015	17417.27	165.65	0.00
12/23/2015	17602.61	185.34	0.00
12/24/2015	17552.17	0.00	50.44
12/28/2015	17528.27	0.00	23.90
12/29/2015	17720.98	192.71	0.00
12/30/2015	17603.87	0.00	117.11
12/31/2015	17425.03	0.00	178.84
1/4/2016	17148.94	0.00	276.09
1/5/2016	17158.66	9.72	0.00
1/6/2016	16906.51	0.00	252.15
1/7/2016	16514.1	0.00	392.41
1/8/2016	16346.45	0.00	167.65
1/11/2015	16398.57	52.12	0.00
1/12/2016	16516.22	117.65	0.00
1/13/2016	16151.41	0.00	364.81
1/14/2016	16379.05	227.64	0.00
1/15/2016	15988.08	0.00	390.97
1/19/2016	16016.02	27.94	0.00
1/20/2016	15766.74	0.00	249.28
1/21/2016	15882.68	115.94	0.00

Price Momentum

Formula

$$M = V - VX$$

Where V is the latest price, VX is the closing price X number of days ago

Overview

One of the strengths of price momentum, is it provides good insight on major moves in the market or in a stock unless the move whip saw up or down.

Interpretation

The moment of a stock is the differences between the price of a stock now and the price of a stock several periods ago. That period can change depending on the trend you wish to track. The momentum will indicate how fast the stock or issue is moving upwards (bullish) or downwards (bearish). When the momentum of a stock or issue starts to increase, the stock or issue should move in an upwards direction and if the momentum fails the stock or issue should start to decrease or fail.

Example

On the chart on the next page we have an example of price momentum and the NASDAQ, from 5/19/16 to 8/18/16. On the price momentum chart there are two examples of the NASDAQ reaching highs and lows of the trend. The green area are the high and the red is the low of the trend, the yellow area is the up and down indicator for the price momentum formula we receive from stock charts .com. On 5/19/16 the NASDAQ hit the low of the trend while the price momentum continued down until 5/26/16 when the price momentum turned up and continued up to 6/13/16 even when the NASDAC turned down on 6/8/16. On 6/27/16 the price momentum indicator turned up and ran up to 8/17/16 two days after the market hit the high on 8/15/16. As you can see on the chart the price momentum started to waiver on 8/3/16, 8/9/16 and 8/11/16. The price momentum indicator as you can see on the chart on the next page will keep you on the correct side of the trend. It is not a lead indicator, but it is a helpful tool. We never use one indicator or one formula to invest or track the market always use multiple indicators and formulas to ensure a major trend and eliminate investing in a minor trend.

NASDAC	DATE	UP	DOWN
4712.53	5/19/2016		1
4769.56	5/20/2016		1
4765.78	5/23/2016		1
4861.06	5/24/2016		1
4901.77	5/25/2016	1	
4933.5	5/27/2016	1	
4948.06	5/31/2016	1	
4952.25	6/1/2016	1	
4971.36	6/2/2016	1	
4942.52	6/3/2016	1	
4968.71	6/6/2016	1	
4961.75	6/7/2016	1	
4974.64	6/8/2016	1	
4958.62	6/9/2016	1	
4894.55	6/10/2016	1	
4844.94	6/13/2016	1	
4843.55	6/13/2016	1	
4834.93	6/14/2016		1
4844.92	6/16/2016		1
4800.34	6/17/2016		1
4837.21	6/20/2016		1
4843.76	6/21/2016		1
4833.32	6/22/2016		1
4910.04	6/23/2016		1
4707.98	6/24/2016		1
4594.44	6/27/2016		1
4691.87	6/28/2016		1
4779.25	6/29/2016		1
4842.67	6/30/2016		1
4862.57	7/1/2016		1
4822.9	7/5/2016		1
4869.16	7/6/2016		1
4878.81	7/7/2016		1
4956.76	7/8/2016	1	
4988.64	7/11/2016	1	
5022.82	7/12/2016	1	
5005.73	7/13/2016	1	
5034.06	7/14/2016	1	
5029	7/15/2016	1	
5055.78	7/18/2016	1	
5036.37	7/19/2016	1	
5073.93	7/20/2016	1	
5089.93	7/21/2016	1	
5100.16	7/22/2016	1	
5097.63	7/25/2016	1	
5110.05	7/26/2016	1	
5139.81	7/27/2016	1	
5154.98	7/28/2016	1	
5162.13	7/29/2016	1	
5184.2	8/1/2016	1	
5137.73	8/2/2016	1	
5159.74	8/3/2016		1
5166.25	8/4/2016	1	
5221.12	8/5/2016	1	
5213.14	8/8/2016	1	
5225.48	8/9/2016		1
5204.58	8/10/2016	1	
5228.4	8/11/2016		1
5232.9	8/12/2016	1	
5262.02	8/15/2016	1	
5227.11	8/16/2016	1	
5228.66	8/17/2016	1	
5240.15	8/18/2016		1

Pring's Know Sure Thing

Formula

RCMA1= 10-periods simple moving average of 10-period rate of change

RCMA2= 10-periods simple moving average of 15-period rate of change

RCMA3= 10-periods simple moving average of 20-period rate of change

RCMA4= 10-periods simple moving average of 30-period rate of change

KST = (RCMA1 x1) + (RCMA2x2) + (RCMA3 x3) + (RCMA4x 4)

Signal line = 9 – period SMA OF KST

Overview

Pring's Know Sure Thing (KST) is a momentum oscillator based on the smoothed rate of change for four different time frames. The (KST) provides signals for overbought/ oversold crossovers and convergence/ divergences, it can also be used just like any momentum oscillator. The Pring's Know Sure Thing was developed by Martin Pring in 1992.

Interpretation

The Pring's Know Sure Thing simply can be used as a bull / bear indicator by plotting a zero base line and when the (KST) moves above the base line the trend is bullish and when it moves below the base line the trend is bearish. The Pring's Know Sure Thing that we like to use is the crossover, as the (KST) cross in an upwards direction the market should move up and when it crosses in a downwards direction the market should move downward.

Example

The Pring's Know Sure Thing as you can see, in the example on the next page, does not give, the high or the low of an issue, but it can keep you on the right side of the issue. On 6/25/16 the NASDAC hit a low of 4594.44 as the Pring's Know Sure Thing continued down to 7/11/16 when it turned up after the NASDAQ move 394 points from the low of the trend. The (KST) continued an upwards trend until 8/18/16 after a 252 point move up. The NASDAQ continued to move up and down until it hit the high of the trend on 9/7/16 at 5283.93 43.78 point higher then when the (KST) turned down. The (KST) provided a good signal to exit the NASDAQ before the trend changed direction. We never use one indicator or one formula to invest or track the market always use multiple indicators and formulas to ensure a major trend and eliminate investing in a minor trend.

pring's sure thing	date	close	up	down
	6/25/2016	4594.44		1
	6/28/2016	4691.87		1
	6/29/2016	4779.25		1
	6/30/2016	4842.57		1
	7/1/2016	4862.57		1
	7/5/2016	4822.9		1
	7/6/2016	4859.16		1
	7/7/2016	4876.81		1
	7/8/2016	4956.76		1
	7/11/2016	4988.64	1	
	7/12/2016	5022.82	1	
	7/13/2016	5005.73	1	
	7/14/2016	5034.06	1	
	7/15/2016	5029	1	
	7/18/2016	5055.78	1	
	7/19/2016	5036.37	1	
	7/20/2016	5073.93	1	
	7/21/2016	5089.93	1	
	7/22/2016	5100.16	1	
	7/25/2016	5097.63	1	
	7/26/2016	5110.05	1	
	7/27/2016	5139.81	1	
	7/28/2016	5154.98	1	
	7/29/2016	5162.13	1	
	8/1/2016	5184.2	1	
	8/2/2016	5137.73	1	
	8/3/2016	5159.74	1	
	8/4/2016	5166.25	1	
	8/5/2016	5221.12	1	
	8/8/2016	5213.14	1	
	8/9/2016	5225.48	1	
	8/10/2016	5204.58	1	
	8/11/2016	5228.4	1	
	8/12/2016	5232.9	1	
	8/15/2016	5262.02	1	
	8/16/2016	5227.11	1	
	8/17/2016	5228.66	1	
	8/18/2016	5240.15		1
	8/19/2016	5238.38		1
	8/22/2016	5244.6		1
	8/23/2016	5260.08		1
	8/24/2016	5217.69		1
	8/25/2016	5212.2		1
	8/26/2016	5218.92		1
	8/29/2016	5232.33		1
	8/30/2016	5222.99		1
	8/31/2016	5213.22		1
	9/1/2016	5227.21		1
	9/2/2016	5249.9		1
	9/6/2016	5275.91		1
	9/7/2016	5283.93		1
	9/8/2016	5259.48		1
	9/9/2016	5125.91		1
	9/12/2016	5211.89		1
	9/13/2016	5155.25		1
	9/14/2016	5173.77		1

Rate of Change

Formula

ROC = (close − close n periods ago) / (close n periods ago) * 100

Overview

The Rate of Change indicator is simply a momentum oscillator that compares the close of an issue to the close of n periods ago. The Rate of Change oscillator (ROC) identifies overbought or oversold issues, and it also provides the trend of the market or issue. The (ROC) can be plotted by using a zero baseline, as the (ROC) moves above zero the trend is bullish and when it moves below zero the trend is bearish. The rate of change will indicate extreme bullish and bearish signals, providing a signal to buy or sell. When the (ROC) indicates an extreme bearish signal, the issue should turn bullish and vice a versa if the (ROC) is indicating an extreme bullish signal the issue should turn bearish, however the market or issue can stay overbought or oversold for an extended period.

Interpretation

The Rate of Change indicator is purely a momentum indicator. The (ROC) has no limits in the positive range but does have a limit in the negative range. The market or issue can only decline 100% or to zero.

The Rate of Change can be misleading in some cases, if the issues makes a sharp upwards or downwards turn it will provide a false reading of either a bullish or bearish signal. There is one key indicator to remember if the Rate of Change oscillator is in a positive range the issue or market is increasing. One of the most popular time frame to use is the 12day rate of change oscillator, by using zero, as a cross over signal, the rate of change will keep you on the right side of the market or issue. The (ROC) can be set below behind or above the market or issue to provide a more sensitive signal or trigger. The Rate of Change provides signals for overbought over sold and the overall trend of the market or issue.

Example

On the chart on the next page you can see an example of the Rate of Change, with the S&P 500. On 6/24/16 the (ROC) turned down two days before the market hit its low of the trend. On 6/25/16 the S&P hit the low of the trend and the (ROC) the next day is showing an uptrend for the next four days. On 7/22/16 the S&P500 hit its high of the trend and the Rate of Change oscillator is showing a down signal, it continued down for the next four day. The (ROC) indicator fluctuates a lot as you can see on the chart, but in both trend reversals the (ROC) had a good signal in the correct direction for several days. We never use one indicator or one formula to invest or track the market always use multiple indicators and formulas to ensure a major trend and eliminate investing in a minor trend.

DATE	CLOSE	roc	up	down
6/20/2016	2083.25		1	
6/21/2016	2088.9		1	
6/22/2016	2085.46			1
6/23/2016	2113.32		1	
6/24/2016	2037.41			1
6/25/2016	2000.54			1
6/28/2016	2036.09		1	
6/29/2016	2070.77		1	
6/30/2016	2098.94		1	
7/1/2016	2102.95		1	
7/5/2016	2088.55			1
7/6/2016	2099.73		1	
7/7/2016	2097.9			1
7/8/2016	2129.9		1	
7/11/2016	2137.16		1	
7/12/2016	2152.14			1
7/13/2016	2152.43		1	
7/14/2015	2163.75		1	
7/15/2016	2161.74			1
7/18/2016	2166.89			1
7/19/2016	2163.78			1
7/20/2016	2173		1	
7/21/2016	2165.17		1	
7/22/2016	2175.03			1
7/25/2016	2168.48			1
7/26/2016	2169.18			1
7/27/2016	2166.58			1
7/28/2016	2170.06			1

Relative Strength Index

Formula;

100-(100/((up/down)+1))

RSI 9 day = 100-(100/ (sum of price change for up for the last 9 days/ sum of the price change down for the last 9 days +1))

RSI 14 day =100-(100/ (sum of price change for up the last 14 days/ sum of the price change down for the last 14 days +1))

Overview

The Relative Strength Index (RSI) that we use, takes the moving averages of the up days and the down days and then dividing the two, to format a number between zero and one hundred. The relative strength can be calculated by using any duration of days, the number of days we use is 9 days for the short term and 14 days for the long term. The Relative Strength Index was developed by J Welles Wilder and published in 1978 and is one of the most popular oscillator indices.

The (RSI) compares the price strength of an index or security, and there are several signals and triggers the formula provides, tops and bottoms, support and resistance, divergence and bullish and bearish signals.

Interpretation

The Relative Strength Index separates the number of up days and the number of down days and the strength of each move, by using an exponential moving average (EMA) and then plotting the number from zero to one hundred in our formula. The triggers and signals are a little different in our formula then in J Welles Wilder formula. Our formula has multiple signals and they are as follows. Over bought is when the issue crosses over 80, and when the issue crosses below 20 it is oversold. When the issue crosses 65 the issue become bullish and when it crosses below 40 it become bearish. When the 9 day and the 14 day cross, this is a signal of strength or weakness. When the 9 day is higher than the 14 day this is a sign of strength, and weakness when the 14 day is higher than the 9 day. We also have Resistance levels for bullish and bearish signals. Bullish signals 65, 80 90 and bearish signals are 10, 20, 30, and 55, when a level change occurs the next day the price action can be the opposite of the current days price action. The Relative Strength Index can stay over bought or over sold for an extended period, timing is no easily determined.

Example

Relative Strength Index that we designed is a little different from J Welles Wilder formula. The standard RSI formula measures the speed of change, of price momentum by percentage over x amount of days and smoothed by a simple moving average, of 14 days, and oscillates between zero and 100. We have added a twist to the original formula. We added two time periods to our chart a 9 day and 14 day time period and instead of an average of a loss or gain we add the total of up days and down days. On the chart on the next page you can see the 9 day and the 14 day, the triggers for our formula, every time the 9 and 14 day cross we boxed the change, so you could easily see the change in price momentum. On 7/20/16 the 9 day was up 9 continuous days. When this happens, the formula is maxed out at 100 percent, if there are 9 down days the formula will show zero. Looking at the (RSI) on the next page the up down columns show the change between the 9 day and the 14 day. In the market column we install the trend of the market, on 7/29/16 the DOW changed from a bull market to a bear / bull market before changing to a bear market on 8/3/16. This is important because we never want to buy up when the market is falling (bear) or buy down when the market is rising (bull). We want to buy the way the trend is moving at all times. The relative strength of the market or issue is a good tool to keep you on the correct side of the market. We never use one indicator or one formula to invest or track the market always use multiple indicators and formulas to ensure a major trend and eliminate investing in a minor trend.

DATE	CLOSE	POSITIVE	NEGATIVE	9 UP	DOWN	9	14 UP	DOWN	14	MARKET	9	14	up	down
7/20/2016	18595.03	36.02	0.00	699.15	0.00	86.84	1031.84	131.49	88.70		#DIV/0!	88.6971	1	
7/21/2016	18517.23	0.00	77.80	448.29	77.80	85.21	796.53	209.29	79.19		85.2117	79.1921	1	
7/22/2016	18570.85	53.62	0.00	421.72	77.80	84.43	830.77	209.29	79.88		84.4250	79.8771	1	
7/25/2016	18493.06	0.00	77.79	300.98	155.59	65.92	830.77	178.33	82.33		65.9220	82.3278		1
7/26/2016	18473.75	0.00	19.31	276.53	174.90	61.26	752.77	197.64	79.20		61.2565	79.2048		1
7/27/2016	18472.17	0.00	1.58	142.24	176.48	44.63	752.77	176.48	81.01		44.6285	81.0083		1
7/28/2016	18456.35	0.00	15.82	132.10	192.30	40.72	501.91	192.30	72.30		40.7213	72.2994		1
7/29/2016	18432.24	0.00	24.11	115.60	216.41	34.82	421.72	216.41	66.09	bear/bull	34.8182	66.0868		1
8/1/2016	18404.51	0.00	27.73	89.64	244.14	26.86	300.98	244.14	55.21		26.8560	55.2135		1
8/2/2016	18313.77	0.00	90.74	53.62	334.88	13.80	276.53	334.88	45.23		13.8018	45.2282		1
8/3/2016	18355	41.23	0.00	94.85	257.08	26.95	183.47	334.88	35.40	bear	26.9514	35.3950		1
8/4/2016	18325.17	0.00	29.83	41.23	296.01	12.56	176.35	364.71	32.22		12.5648	32.2151		1
8/5/2016	18543	217.83	0.00	259.06	209.12	55.33	374.66	364.71	50.67		55.3334	50.6729	1	
8/8/2016	18529.29	0.00	13.71	259.06	203.52	56.00	348.70	378.42	47.96		56.0033	47.9563	1	
8/9/2016	18533.05	3.76	0.00	262.82	201.94	56.55	316.44	378.42	45.54		56.5496	45.5401	1	
8/10/2016	18495.66	0.00	37.39	262.82	223.51	54.04	316.44	338.01	48.35		54.0415	48.3521	1	
8/11/2016	18613.52	117.86	0.00	380.68	199.40	65.63	380.68	338.01	52.97	bull/bear	65.6254	52.9686	1	
8/12/2016	18576.47	0.00	37.05	380.68	208.72	64.59	380.68	297.27	56.15		64.5877	56.1516	1	
8/15/2016	18636.05	59.58	0.00	440.26	117.98	78.87	440.26	277.96	61.30		78.8657	61.2988	1	
8/16/2016	18552.02	0.00	84.03	399.03	202.01	66.39	440.26	340.41	54.99		66.3899	54.9864	1	
8/17/2016	18573.94	21.92	0.00	420.95	172.18	70.97	462.18	344.59	57.29		70.9710	57.2877	1	
8/18/2016	18597.7	23.76	0.00	226.88	172.18	56.85	485.94	320.48	60.26		56.8536	60.2589		1
8/19/2016	18552.57	0.00	45.13	226.88	203.60	52.70	485.94	337.88	58.99		52.7040	58.9862		1
8/22/2016	18529.42	0.00	23.15	223.12	226.75	49.60	485.94	270.29	64.26		49.5966	64.2582		1
8/23/2016	18547.3	17.88	0.00	241.00	189.36	56.00	462.59	270.29	63.12		55.9996	63.1195		1
8/24/2016	18481.48	0.00	65.82	123.14	255.18	32.55	462.59	306.28	60.16	bear	32.5492	60.1649		1
8/25/2016	18448.41	0.00	33.07	123.14	251.20	32.90	244.76	339.35	41.90		32.8952	41.9031		1
8/26/2016	18395.38	0.00	53.03	63.56	304.23	17.28	244.76	378.67	39.26		17.2816	39.2602		1
8/29/2016	18502.99	107.61	0.00	171.17	220.20	43.74	348.61	378.67	47.93		43.7361	47.9334		1
8/30/2016	18454.3	0.00	48.69	149.25	268.89	35.69	348.61	389.97	47.20		35.6938	47.2000		1
8/31/2016	18400.88	0.00	53.42	125.49	322.31	28.02	230.75	443.39	34.23		28.0237	34.2288		1
9/1/2016	18419.3	18.42	0.00	143.91	277.18	34.18	249.17	406.34	38.01		34.1756	38.0116		1
9/2/2016	18491.96	72.66	0.00	216.57	254.03	46.02	262.25	406.34	39.22		46.0200	39.2243	1	
9/6/2016	18538.12	46.16	0.00	244.85	254.03	49.08	308.41	322.31	48.90		49.0799	48.8981	1	
9/7/2016	18526.14	0.00	11.98	244.85	200.19	55.02	286.49	334.29	46.15		55.0175	46.1500	1	
9/8/2016	18479.91	0.00	46.23	244.85	213.35	53.44	262.73	380.52	40.84		53.4374	40.8442	1	
9/9/2016	18085.45	0.00	394.46	244.85	554.78	30.62	262.73	729.85	26.47		30.6204	26.4694	1	
9/12/2016	18325.07	239.62	0.00	376.86	554.78	40.45	502.35	706.70	41.55		40.4512	41.5492		1
9/13/2016	18066.75	0.00	258.32	376.86	764.41	33.02	484.47	965.02	33.42		33.0211	33.4235		1
9/14/2016	18034.77	0.00	31.98	376.86	742.97	33.65	484.47	931.18	34.22		33.6533	34.2224		1
9/15/2016	18212.48	177.71	0.00	536.15	742.97	41.92	662.18	898.11	42.44		41.9155	42.4395		1
9/16/2016	18123.8	0.00	88.68	463.49	831.65	35.79	662.18	933.76	41.49		35.7869	41.4915		1
9/19/2016	18120.17	0.00	3.63	417.33	835.28	33.32	554.57	937.39	37.17		33.3168	37.1706		1
9/20/2016	18129.96	9.79	0.00	427.12	823.30	34.16	564.36	888.70	38.84		34.1581	38.8394		1
9/21/2016	18293.7	163.74	0.00	590.86	777.07	43.19	728.10	835.28	46.57		43.1937	46.5722		1
9/22/2016	18392.46	98.76	0.00	689.62	382.61	64.32	808.44	835.28	49.18		64.3164	49.1836	1	
9/23/2016	18261.45	0.00	131.01	450.00	513.62	46.70	735.78	966.29	43.23		46.6989	43.2285	1	
9/26/2016	18094	0.00	167.45	450.00	452.78	51.56	689.62	1139.24	37.82		51.5612	37.8214	1	

Stochastic Oscillator

Formula

The 5-period stochastic oscillator in a daily timeframe is defined as follows:

%k = (price −L5) / (H5 − L5)

%D = 100*((K1 + K2+K3) /3)

H5 and L5 are the highest and lowest price in the last 5 days respectively, while %D is the 3-day moving average of %k (the last 3 values of %K/3).

Overview

Stochastic processes were first studied rigorously in the late 19th century to aid in understanding financial markets and Brownian motion. The first person to describe the mathematics behind Brownian motion was Thorvald N. Thiele in a paper on the method of least squares published in 1880. This was followed independently by Louis Bachelier in 1900 in his PhD thesis "The theory of speculation", in which he presented a stochastic analysis of the stock and option markets. Albert Einstein (in one of his 1905 papers) and Marian Smoluchowski (1906) brought the solution of the problem to the attention of physicists and presented it as a way to indirectly confirm the existence of atoms and molecules. Their equations describing Brownian motion were subsequently verified by the experimental work of Jean Baptiste Perrin in 1908. An excerpt from

Einstein's paper describes the fundamentals of a stochastic model: "It must clearly be assumed that each individual particle executes a motion which is independent of the motions of all other particles; it will also be considered that the movements of one and the same particle in different time intervals are independent processes, as long as these time intervals are not chosen too small". In technical analysis of securities trading, the stochastic oscillator is a momentum indicator that use support and resistance levels. Dr. George lane developed this indicator in the late 1950s.

Interpretation

In analyzing the market stochastically, there are several different popular formulas used, slow, fast and full stochastic oscillators. We like the slow oscillator in most cases except, when we are analyzing the (VIX) the volatility index. Then we use the fast stochastic oscillator, due to the fast moving nature of the index. The oscillators range is from 0 to 100, with 80 indicating over bought and 20 indicating over sold. The signal is when the stochastic oscillator shows extreme convergence/divergence, and the trigger is when the oscillator crosses above 80 or below 20. When the oscillators hovers above 80 this means the issue is overbought and should reverse down, and vice a versa, when the oscillator crosses below 20 this means the issue is oversold and the issue show turn up. However, we know that an issue can stay over bought or over sold for an extend length of time.

Example

On the chart on the next page, is an example of the slow stochastic analyzing the NASDAQ index. The column (C/D) is the convergence/divergence of the formula it helps to confirm the strength of the fast and slow indicator of the oscillator, by tracking the convergence/ divergence of the two lines you can see the strength of the formula itself. For example, on 7/31/14 the down ward turn of the Nasdaq convergence / divergence was -18.77 and then started to fade as the NASDAQ index moved to its low giving us a signal that the down turn is coming to the end, as it did on 8/5/14. We never use one indicator or one formula to invest or track the market always use multiple indicators and formulas to insure a major trend and eliminate investing in a minor trend.

Date	CLOSE	fast	slow	c/d	up	down
7/24/2014	4472.11	86.27	74.97	11.3	1	
7/25/2014	4449.56	84.75	81.82	2.93	1	
7/28/2014	4444.91	77.71	82.91	-5.2		1
7/29/2014	4442.7	70.42	77.63	-7.21		1
7/30/2014	4462.9	73.67	73.93	-0.26		1
7/31/2014	4363.39	36.08	54.85	-18.77		1
8/1/2014	4352.64	37.98	55.48	-17.5		1
8/4/2014	4383.89	22.65	38.47	-15.82		1
8/5/2014	4333.58	24.22	28.28	-4.06		1
8/6/2014	4355.05	23.86	24.71	-0.85		1
8/7/2014	4334.97	15.02	21.32	-6.3		1
8/8/2014	4372.9	19.06	19.6	-0.54		1
8/11/2014	4401.33	28.84	20.97	7.87	1	
8/12/2014	4389.25	39.9	29.26	10.64	1	
8/13/2014	4434.13	54.18	40.97	13.21	1	
8/14/2014	4453	66.34	53.47	12.87	1	
8/15/2014	4464.93	82.31	67.61	14.7	1	
8/18/2014	4508.31	91.22	79.96	11.26	1	
8/19/2014	4527.51	95.98	89.84	6.14	1	
8/20/2014	4526.48	98.59	95.27	3.32	1	
8/21/2014	4532.1	98.45	97.68	0.77	1	
8/22/2014	4538.55	97.38	98.14	-0.76		1
8/25/2014	4557.35	96.57	97.47	-0.9		1
8/26/2014	4570.64	96.82	96.54	0.28	1	
8/27/2014	4569.62	96.67	96.49	0.18	1	
8/28/2014	4557.69	95.56	96.15	-0.59		1
9/2/2014	4598.19	96.96	96.24	0.72	1	
9/3/2014	4572.56	93.08	95.42	-2.34		1

Trend

Formula

When the Relative Strength Index reaches 65, we consider that bullish and stays bullish until it passes below 40. When the Relative Strength Index reaches 40, we consider that bearish and stays bearish until it crosses above 65. When the Relative Strength Index reaches 65 and is below 40 we consider that to be bull/bear Signal and vice a versa when it is 40 / 65 we consider that a bear/bull signal. The nine day indictor is the lead indicator or trigger, and the fourteen day is confirmation of the trend.

Overview

Technically analyzing an issue or the market, knowing the trend is a crucial part of trading. Technical analysis assumes the market prices trends and we build our formulas around this assumption. The trend of an issue has become a very popular way to find support /resistance levels, and possible change in direction, but this is merely one tool we use to analyze an issue. One of the most popular ways of finding the trend of a market or issue is a trend line. A trend line is a line that connects two or more point in a straight line either up or down. Up trend line is formed by connecting two or more low point in a positive direction. If the price of the market or issue is above the trend line, this is a signal that the issue is sturdy and intact. Down trend connects two or more high points in a straight line in a negative direction. If the price remains below the down trend line it is considered sturdy and intact. When the market or issue moves above or below the trend line (bullish / bearish) this is a signal that there could be a change in direction. The general rule is that it takes two points to form a trend line and the third point to validate the trend.

Interpretation

The market is comprised of three trends, primary trend secondary trend and minor trend, these trends can be in a bullish or bearish market. Primary trend usually last more than one year and can last for up to several years. A secondary trend is an intermediate corrective reaction to the primary trend typically lasting from one to three month and retraces from 1/3 to 2/3 of the previous movement in the primary trend. A minor trend is a short term movement lasting from one day to three weeks. Secondary trends typically consist of a number of minor trends. Note minor trends can be manipulated to some degree and can be misleading, so minor trends are unimportant to our treading system. Knowing the trend is the key and very important. Primary and secondary trends are what we focus on with this system. Focus on the primary trend as the primary trend will outperform the secondary trend in most cases. The trend of the market is a crucial tool to use, and we never go against the trend of an issue or of the market. When an issue is in a confirmed-up trend never go against the uptrend and vice a versa never go against a down trend, if you stay in the trend of the issue you will have a 70% better chance of having a successful investment.

Example

The example on the next page demonstrates an uptrend, down trend, and a sideways trend. A uptrend is when the lows are higher than the previous lows and the highs are higher than the previous high. A down trend is when highs make lower highs than the previous highs and lower lows than pervious lows. A sideways trend is when the issue moves with in a channel not make new confirmed highs or confirmed new lows. A confirmation of a trend could be when the down trend line crosses the uptrend line for a uptrend buy, and vice a versa for a down trend buy. The chart on the next page reflects a bullish issue, so the primary trend is up, so we would only invest in the uptrend signals.

Trend Lines

True Strength Index

Formula

The true strength index can be divided into three parts :

Double smooth price change

Double smooth absolute price change

TSI formula is the formula we like to use the formula;

TSI = 100 x (double smoothed PC / double smoothed Absolute PC)

Overview

The true strength indicator aids traders in determining the trend of an issue, as well as the overbought and over sold conditions of a security by incorporating purchasing momentum (short term) with the lagging benefits of moving averages

Interpretation

The TSI is a variation of the Relative Strength Index and was developed by William Blau. It uses a differencing function to measure momentum and an averaging function to correlate the momentum to the price trend. In other words, the indicator combines the leading characteristic of a differencing momentum calculation with the lagging characteristic of an averaging function to create an indicator that reflects price direction and is in sync with market turns.

Example

On the chart on the next page you can see an example of the True Strength Index daily position either up or down for the day. We get this information daily, from stock charts .com this is a great place to get your daily numbers and info, and it is totally free. There are three moves in the chart on the next page two highs and one low.

DATE	CLOSE	total up	total down	c/d	up %	true strength index	up	down
3/1/2017	21,115.55	18	1	17	95%		1	
2/28/2017	20,812.24	11	8	3	58%		1	
2/27/2017	20,837.44	13	6	7	68%		1	
2/24/2017	20,821.76	12	7	5	63%		1	
2/23/2017	20810.32	14	5	9	74%		1	
2/22/2017	20775.6	14	5	9	74%		1	
2/21/2017	20743	18	1	17	95%		1	
2/17/2017	20624.05	13	6	7	68%		1	
2/16/2017	20619.77	15	4	11	79%		1	
2/15/2017	20611.86	19	0	19	100%		1	
2/14/2017	20504.41	17	2	15	89%		1	
2/13/2017	20412.16	18	1	17	95%		1	
2/10/2017	20269.37	14	4	10	78%		1	
2/9/2017	20172.4	10	8	2	56%		1	
2/8/2017	20054.34	7	11	-4	39%			1
2/7/2017	20068.68	10	8	2	56%			1
2/6/2017	20052.42	8	10	-2	44%			1
2/3/2017	20071.46	13	5	8	72%			1
2/2/2017	19884.91	6	12	-6	33%			1
2/1/2017	19890.94	9	9	0	50%			1
1/31/2017	19864.09	8	10	-2	44%			1
1/30/2017	19971.13	6	12	-6	33%			1
1/27/2017	20093.78	9	9	0	50%		1	
1/26/2017	20100.92	13	5	8	72%			1
1/25/2017	20068.51	13	5	8	72%			1
1/24/2017	19912.71	12	6	6	67%			1
1/20/2017	19827.25	7	11	-4	39%			1
1/19/2017	19732.4	1	17	-16	6%			1
1/18/2017	19804.72	4	14	-10	22%			1
1/17/2017	19826.77	4	14	-10	22%			1
1/13/2017	19885.73	4	14	-10	22%			1
1/12/2017	19891	3	15	-12	17%			1
1/11/2017	19954.28	10	8	2	56%			1
1/10/2017	19855.53	1	17	-16	6%			1
1/7/2017	19887.38	3	15	-12	17%			1

VOLATILITY

Formula

The formula for the CBOE VIX is extremely complicated. For an insight on a general example go to Investopedia .com they provide a calculation that can be studied.

Overview

In general, the volatility index is also known as the fear factor. When the volatility moves up there is more uncertainty in the market or issue and when the volatility is low there is more stability in the market or issue.

Interpretation

Volatility expresses the amount of uncertainty or risk in the market. When the market has high volatility, this mean the market can change considerably over a short period of time in either direction. A low volatility means the market or issue moves at a steady pace over a certain time period, meaning the market does not fluctuate dramatically

Example

On the example on the next page we can see a chart of the S&P and the VIX in direct correlation with each other. We can see the VIX moving down as the S&P is moving up. The S&P hit a high on 6/8/16 as the VIX was falling to its low of 13.47 3 days before the S&P hit its high.

The c/d is the trigger for our formula as you can see, as the VIX goes up the market moves down and as the VIX moves down the market moves up. When fear creeps into the market place the market drops, and when the market place is calm the market move up. We never just use one formula to invest the multi formula system will smooth out the whip saws and give us a better insight on the direction of the market or issue.

date	s&p	vix	up	down	c/d	%
5/16/2016	2066.66	14.68	9	4	5	69%
5/17/2016	2047.21	14.78	9	4	5	69%
5/18/2016	2047.63	15.95	10	3	7	77%
5/19/2016	2040.04	16.33	11	2	9	85%
5/20/2016	2052.32	15.2	8	5	3	62%
5/23/2016	2048.04	15.82	10	3	7	77%
5/24/2016	2076.06	14.42	7	6	1	54%
5/26/2016	2090.1	13.42	2	11	-9	15%
5/27/2016	2099.06	13.12	0	13	-13	0%
5/31/2016	2096.96	14.19	5	8	-3	38%
6/1/2016	2099.33	14.2	5	8	-3	38%
6/2/2016	2105.26	13.63	0	13	-13	0%
6/3/2016	2099.13	13.47	2	11	-9	15%
6/6/2014	2109	13.65	3	10	-7	23%
6/7/2016	2112.13	14.05	4	9	-5	31%
6/8/2016	2119.12	14.08	6	7	-1	46%
6/9/2016	2115.48	14.64	10	3	7	77%
6/10/2016	2096.07	17.03	13	1	12	93%
6/13/2016	2079.06	20.97	13	1	12	93%
6/14/2016	2075.32	20.5	9	5	4	64%
6/15/2016	2071.5	20.14	9	5	4	64%
6/16/2016	2077.99	19.63	8	6	2	57%
6/17/2016	2071.22	19.41	7	7	0	50%
6/20/2016	2083.25	18.37	7	6	1	54%
6/21/2016	2088.9	18.48	8	5	3	62%
6/22/2016	2085.46	21.17	10	4	6	71%
6/23/2016	2113.32	17.25	6	7	-1	46%
6/24/2016	2037.41	25.76	12	2	10	86%
6/25/2016	2000.54	23.85	7	7	0	50%
6/28/2016	2036.09	18.75	4	10	-6	29%
6/29/2016	2070.77	16.64	2	11	-9	15%
6/30/2016	2098.94	15.63	0	13	-13	0%

Volume

Formula

There are many ways to calculate volume;

Volume by price, advancing declining volume, Percentage volume oscillator On balance volume, just to name a few. The simplest way to track volume is by the number of contracts purchased for the market or issue if there are 100 trades the volume is 100.

Overview

For every buyer, there is a seller and every transaction impacts the total volume of a period. Volume is the number of contracts traded in the market or an issue at any given period. Volume can be tracked hourly, daily, weekly, monthly. Volume is one of the most important indicators of strength or weakness in the market or issue

Interpretation

One of the best ways to track volume is using a bar chart. When volume is trending up and the market is moving up this is a bullish signal, and when the market is moving down on high volume this is a bearish signal. When the market is moving up or down on low volume this means the move is not strong and the direction could be coming to an end. When buyers and sellers are active at a certain price point the volume level rises. When we look for buy and sell points volume levels can provide clues, to when to buy or when to sell. In short when volume levels are weak, and the markets are moving in either direction there is a good chance the market or issue could change in direction

Example

In the example on the next page we can see volume in medium to high levels as the S&P hits a low on high volume 8/18/17, and then turns up on high volume. We can see 16 positive days on medium to high volume compared to 4 down days on medium volume. We never use one formula to invest in the market we always use multiple formulas before investing.

DATE	CLOSE	total up	total down	volume	up	down
9/18/2017	2503.87	15	5	med	1	0
9/15/2017	2500.23	14	6	high	1	0
9/14/2017	2495.62	14	6	med	0	1
9/13/2017	2498.37	15	5	med	1	0
9/12/2017	2496.48	18	2	med	1	0
9/11/2017	2488.11	18	2	med	1	0
9/8/2017	2461.43	10	10	med	0	1
9/7/2017	2465.1	11	9	high	1	0
9/6/2017	2465.54	17	3	med	1	0
9/5/2017	2457.57	11	9	high	1	0
9/1/2017	2476.55	13	7	med	1	0
8/31/2017	2471.65	15	5	med	1	0
8/30/2017	2457.59	12	8	med	1	0
8/29/2017	2446.3	9	11	med	1	0
8/28/2017	2444.24	7	13	med	1	0
8/25/2017	2443.05	3	17	med	1	0
8/24/2017	2438.97	3	17	med	0	1
8/23/2017	2444.04	5	15	med	0	1
8/22/2017	2452.51	12	8	med	1	0
8/21/2017	2428.37	6	14	med	1	0
8/18/2017	2425.55	3	17	high	1	0
8/17/2017	2430.01	3	17	high	1	0
8/16/2017	2468.11	10	10	med	1	0
8/15/2017	2464.61	7	13	med	0	1
8/14/2017	2465.23	7	13	med	1	0
8/11/2017	2441.32	4	16	med	1	0
8/10/2017	2438.21	4	16	med	0	1
8/9/2017	2474.02	7	13	med	0	1

Pivot Points

Formula

Resistance level 1 = (2xpivot point) − previous low

Support level 1 = (2x pivot point) − previous high

Resistance level 2= (pivot point-support level1) +resistance level 1

= pivot point − (previous high − previous low)

Support level 2 =pivot point- (resistance level 1- support level 1)

= pivot point- (previous high − previous low)

Resistance level 3 = (pivot point-support level2) + resistance level 2

=previous high + 2 (pivot point − low)

Support level 3 = pivot point − (resistance level 2- support level 2)

= previous low-2(previous high- pivot point)

Overview

A pivot point is a technical indicator that determines the overall trend of the market of a select time frame. Simply put a pivot point is the average of the high low and the closing price from the previous trading day. Generally, when the market is trading above the pivot point this indicates the market is bullish and when the market crosses below the pivot point this is a bearish signal

Interpretation

Pivot points are commonly used for trading stocks commodities and futures.

The pivot points are fixed from the day before and are used as support and resistance levels R1 and R2 are the high resistance levels and S1 and S2 are the lower support levels. Traders sometimes use pivot points to place a sell order as the market drops to a support level and a buy order when the market breaks through a resistance level. To increase confirmation of a pivot point support or resistance level one should use moving averages and trend line in conjunction with the pivot points to enhance the probability of the direction of the move.

Example

On the chart on the next page you can see the pivot point levels move up and down as the NASDAQ moves up and down. On 9/27/17 the pivot points change direction from R1 to P to P to R1 then breaks through on 10/5/17, the R1 support level. Looking at the chart on 10/13/17 the NASDAQ moves through the R2 support level as the market move upwards in a bullish trend. From 9/14/17 to 10/13/17 the NASDAQ move 176 points up as the market moved through the resistance level to confirm a bullish trend.

DATE	CLOSE	pivots	location	up	down
10/13/2017	6,605.80		r2	1	
10/12/2017	6,591.51		r1r2	1	
10/11/2017	6,603.55		r1r2	1	
10/10/2017	6,587.25		r1r2	1	
10/9/2017	6,579.73		r1r2	1	
10/6/2017	6,590.18		r1r2	1	
10/5/2017	6,585.36		r1r2	1	
10/4/2017	6,534.63		pr1	1	
10/3/2017	6,531.71		pr1	1	
10/2/2017	6,516.72		pr1	1	
9/29/2017	6,495.96		pr1	1	
9/28/2017	6,453.45		pr1	1	
9/27/2017	6,453.26		pr1	1	
9/26/2017	6,380.16		r1p		1
9/25/2017	6,370.59		r1p		1
9/22/2017	6,426.92		r1p		1
9/21/2017	6,422.69		pr1	1	
9/20/2017	6,456.04		pr1	1	
9/19/2017	6,461.32		pr1	1	
9/18/2017	6,454.64		pr1	1	
9/15/2017	6,448.47		pr1	1	
9/14/2017	6,429.08		pr1		1

FIBONACCI

Formula

The Fibonacci formula extends to infinity, however listed below is an example of the sequence;

Each number after 0, and 1, is the sum of the two prior numbers (1+2=3, 2+3=5, 5+8=13,8+13=21 and so on)

Retracement numbers are found by;

1: Dividing a number by the previous number which approximates 1.618 (21/13 = 1.6153, 34/21= 1.6190 55/34=1.6176)

2: Dividing a number by the next highest number approximates. .6180

3: Dividing a number by the number two places higher approximates. 3820

4: Dividing a number by the number three places higher approximates. 2360

Fan lines are based on the Fibonacci retracement points and extend up from a trough, the trend lines pass through retracement based on the advance. The points we use in our formula are .236, .382, .5, .618. 1 1.618.

Overview

Leonardo Pisano Bogollo was an Italian mathematician from (1170 – 1250) who lived in Pisa Italy and is credited with, introducing the Fibonacci sequence to the west. In the Fibonacci sequence there is a number that is considered the golden ratio or the golden mean this is 1.618 and can also be called the Phi. The opposite of 1.618 is .618 and these ratios can be found throughout nature, a snail's shell, sunflowers, and the spiral galaxies of outer space.

Interpretation

The Fibonacci formula has a wide array of applications and systems that can be used, for example; Fibonacci retracements, using ratios to identify potential reversal points. Fibonacci fans, based on the retracement points used as trend line extending up and or down to find support levels, retracement points and potential reversal zones. Fibonacci arcs, they are half circles that extend out from a trend line, the arcs add a time element to the retracements. The most popular Fibonacci time zones are 21,34,55,89,144, the theory resembles reversal points and can be found looking ahead at these signals.

Example

For our system we do not use the Fibonacci as a daily signal. We us it to find bullish and bearish support and resistance levels. The top chart is an example of the Fibonacci being used as a potential support levels for a bullish move. On 11/3/15 the Dow jones was 17918.15 and dropped to 17245.20 on 11/13/15. On 12/1/15 the Dow jones hit its high for the trend at 17888.35 which was in between the Fibonacci level of .0618 and 1 after moving through four levels of .236,.382,.5, and .618, on the same chart on the lower left you can see the poivoit points, the move went through two pivot points before failing between p and r1. We like to use the Fibonacci and the pivot point in conjunction with each other to find our support levels. The chart on the next page shows a retracement of the Dow Jones on 12/18/2015 the Dow Jones hit the low of the trend just after the retracement level of 1 and above 1.618. the pivot point level was between s1 and s2. Looking at the charts the Fibonacci and the pivot point have a few levels in common which could be a good support level to keep an eye on. We always want to use multiply systems and formulas to enhance our chance of making the right decision.

Date	Value	Date	Value	Label	Value		Ratio		
11/24/2015	17,812.19	11/3/2015	17,918.15						
11/25/2015	17,813.39	11/13/2015	17,245.20						
11/27/2015	17,798.49			move	672.95	8			
11/30/2015	17,719.92								
12/1/2015	17,888.35			r2	18,945.35		0.236	158.82	17,404.02
12/2/2015	17,729.68			r1	18,304.45		0.382	257.07	17,502.27
12/3/2015	17,477.67			p	17,159.05		0.5	336.48	17,581.68
12/4/2015	17,847.63			s1	16,518.14		0.618	415.88	17,661.08
12/7/2015	17,730.51			s2	15,372.75		0.1	67.30	17,312.50
12/8/2015	17,568.00						1.618	1,088.83	18,334.03
12/9/2015	17,492.30								

Date	Value	Date	Value	Label	Value		Ratio	Diff	Level
12/10/2015	17,574.75	12/1/2015	17,888.35				0.236	151.78	17,736.57
12/11/2015	17,265.27	11/13/2015	17,245.20				0.382	245.68	17,642.67
12/14/2015	17,368.50			move	643.15	12	0.5	321.57	17,566.78
12/15/2015	17,524.91						0.618	397.47	17,490.88
12/16/2015	17,749.09			r2	18,403.49		0.1	64.31	17,824.04
12/17/2015	17,495.84			r1	18,061.70		1.618	1,040.62	16,847.73
12/18/2015	17,128.55			p	17,636.07		2.618	1,683.77	16,204.58
12/20/2015	17,251.62			s1	17,294.28		4.236	2,724.38	15,163.97
12/21/2015	17,417.27			s2	16,868.65				
12/22/2015	17,417.27								
12/23/2015	17,602.61								

Stock Check List

One of the most important things in trading and investing is timing getting in and out at the right time. The most difficult process is trying to pick the top or the bottom of the market or issue. This is virtually impossible to do, so what we try to do, is acquire 80% of the move either up or down depending on the major trend of the market or issue. How do we do this? First, we start by analyzing the stock or market, we want to invest in. On the next page we have a chart to help us pick a stock that has a strong trend up or down. One of the most important things is to invest the same way the markets are moving. If we are in a bull market, we want to wait for a secondary pull back and then invest bullish on our stock or market. By doing this, it will increase our chance of making a profitable investment.

The stock check list will help us determine whether a stock is a good choice to invest in. first select a stock, then complete the checklist. Now this process could take several picks before we find a good stock. To increase your chances of picking a wining stock, select a stock that is in the top five sectors in the market at the time. Second look for sector leaders these are the top stocks in their sector. Next look at stocks that are in the top 50 categories, big cap 20, world leaders, in the IBD, investor's business daily. A stock that is in multiple categories suggest that the stock is strong selection.

The stock check list on the next page can be filled out relatively easily. Start from the top date and price is self-explanatory. The next four lines are the high and low of the stock and the dates this occurred, this is important because we want to see if the stock is close to new highs or lows. The next two lines are making new highs and general market. Making new highs means the stock is higher than the previous high. General market means what is the market doing? What trend are we in, primary secondary or minor. Again, we want to be in the primary market trend. the next fifteen lines are our formulas that we use to track the strength of the stock we can get all this information from stock charts .com for free. Trend lines, accumulation distribution, slow stochastic, Prings Know Sure Thing, Chaikin money flow, money flow rate of change, average directional movement, true strength, commodity channel index, MACD, Relative Strength Index, price momentum. the next three lines are the moving averages we like to look at the 20, 50,100, day. The next line is volume we are looking for positive price momentum, medium to high volume. The next five lines are the pivot points of the stock r2, r1, pivot, s1 s2. Determining where the stock price is in relation to the pivot points gives an indication of the direction for the stock, note if the current price is above the pivot point that is a positive signal. The next section is the rating of the stock, composite rating, (eps) earnings per share rating, relative strength rating, sales margins and rate on equity (smr) rating accumulation and distribution rating, annual rate of return (roe) industry group rating, all of this can be found easily in the IBD. Next, we have the Fibonacci retracement levels, the high the low, price earnings ratio (p/e), and earning per share (eps). At the bottom of the page we have a total of buy and sell signals and a total percentage of a buy signals, if the percent is over 66% this could be something to invest in.

MRNA	PRICE	0.87			BUY	SELL
MARINA BIOTECH INC						
	HIGH	LOW				
FEBUARY HIGH	1.6					
JULY LOW		0.5				
SEPTEMBER HIGH	1.2					
OCTOBER LOW		0.68				
FAILED TO MAKE NEW HIGH						1
TREND LINE		down				1
	FAST	SLOW				
SLOW STOCHASTIC	66.67	72.41				1
PRINGS KNOW SURE THING	-81.77	-158.74			1	
CHAIKIN MONEY FLOW	0.151				1	
PAROBOLIC SAR	10 UP				1	
BOLLINGER BANDS	0.96	0.68			1	
MONEY FLOW	43.39				1	
RATE OF CHANGE	18.57				1	
AVERAGE DIRECTIONAL MOVEMENT	21.06	21.94	27.17			1
TRUE STRENGTH	-1.67	-4.87			1	
COMMODITY CHANNEL INDEX	31.28					1
MACD	0.004	-0.014	0.011		1	
RSI	47.62	47.62				1
PRICE MOMENTUM	1.65	0.84			1	
MOVING AVERAGE 50	0.94					1
MOVING AVERAGE 100	0.78				1	
VOLUME	1760					1
PIVOT POINTS						1
R2	1.14					
R1	1.01					
PIVOT	0.83	RANGE				1
S1	0.70					
S2	0.53					
FIBONACCI						1
SEPTEMBER HIGH	1.2	23.6	0.12	0.80		
OCTOBER LOW	0.68	38.2	0.20	0.88		
DOWN TURN	0.52	50	0.26	0.94		
WE ARE IN THE GREEN		61.8	0.32	1.00		
FIBONACCI 38.2		100	0.52	1.20		
		161.8	0.84	1.52		
		261.8	1.36	2.04		

THE STOCK MADE ITS HIGH FOR THE YEAR BACK IN FEBUARY AT 1.60 IN OCTOBER IT MADE A MOVE UP TO 1.20 WAY SHORT OF THE HIGH FOR THE YEAR MEANING THE STOCK MOVED FROM AN UP TREND TO A DOWNWARD TREND. THE STOCK IS ON A UPWARD TREND NOW BUT IT IS THE SECONDARY TREND NOT THE PRIMARY TREND THE PRIMARY TREND IS DOWN UNTILL IT CLEARS THE FEBUARY HIGH OF 1.60

NOTE :
IF YOU LIKE THIS STOCK A GOOD BUY POINT WOULD BE :

PIVOT POINT S1 AT .70 OR S2 .53
THE STOCK SHOULD TURN DOWN AFTER HITTING ONE OF THE FIBONACCI POINTS ABOVE , WE ARE AT FIBONACCI .382 (STOCK PRICE .87)NOW IF THE STOCK GOES THROUGH THIS POINT THE NEXT RESISSTANCE POINT WOULD BE FIBONACCI .50 (STOCK PRICE .94) THE STOCK NEED TO CLEAR 1.20 FOR THE STOCK TO BE BULLISH (BUY) NOW THE STOCK IS BEARISH (SELL) I TECHNICALLY ANALYZED THIS STOCK FOR THE SHORT TERM WE CAN LOOK AT IT AGAIN BUT FOR NOW IT IS NOT A BUY ..

				TOTAL BUY SELL	10	11
				TOTAL BUY		48%

What are options?

Options are contracts that are traded like stocks. You can buy them through brokers (full-service or online). The value of an option is derived (thus the term derivative is used to classify options) from an underlying security (ie. the option value is based on the value of another investment).

In the case of stock options, the option value is related to the value of the stock the option is associated with. So an option on Apple (AAPL) stock would change in value based on the change in Apple's stock price.

The change in stock price is only one component of an option's value. The option price is also affected by time (options have an expiration, and the closer to this expiration the lower this value becomes) and by the agreed upon price for the contract (more on that below).

DEFINITION: Option - is a contract between two parties to exchange a stock at an agreed upon price (Strike Price) by an agreed upon date (Expiration Date). One party pays for the rights and the other party collects that payment and agrees to commit to the transaction.

The reason it is called an option is that the party who pays for the rights has a choice to go forward with the contract or not. If the party elects to not go forward, they give up the amount they have paid, but have no further obligations. The party that collects the payment does not have this choice. They must comply with whatever the purchaser chooses.

Why should I look at options for investing?

Options offer a greater reward than stocks, but also experience higher risk. A value of an option can increase/decrease 50-100% within days, even if the stock it is associated with moves only a few percent.

For someone who follows investing closely, options can be a great tool to enhance the returns on your portfolio.

Example: If you own 100 shares of Microsoft (MSFT) stock, and you believe the price is going to go up in the short-term. If MSFT is trading at $50/share, and you wanted to increase your holdings to take advantage of the stock price going up, to purchase another 100 shares would cost you $5,000.

However, you could purchase an option (CALL Option) that gives you the right to buy MSFT at $50/share until the 3rd FRI in April (APR CALL contract). This contract might cost $1.00/share, and each contract is for 100 shares. So, to get the same benefit of owning 100 shares, you could buy 1 Call contract for a cost of $100.

Now, if the price of MSFT goes up, the value of this contract will go up. AND, if the price of MSFT goes down, the value of this contract will go down. The most you could lose is the $100 you paid, but if the price of MSFT goes up, you get the benefit of the price increase on 100 shares, without putting up $5,000.

So, if you are interested in investing, and are good at predicting the direction a stock price is headed, options offer a terrific way to enhance the results in your portfolio, without using too much capital.

CALL Options

A CALL Option gives the buyer the right to buy a stock at a set price (Strike Price) within a set time frame (until the Expiration).

Example: A CALL $42 MSFT APR $1.25. This is a contract that gives the buyer the right to buy MSFT at $42 per share (agreed upon Strike Price) by the 3rd Friday in April (Expiration Date).

In the above example, MSFT is trading at $42.80 and there are 28 days until expiration. So, why would someone sell the right to buy MSFT shares at $42.00 when MSFT is already trading at $42.80? Well, the $1.25 that it would cost the buyer is the option price, and that goes to the seller (or what is referred to as the Writer - as they are WRITING the contract). In this case, the writer is willing to sell a contract and collect the $1.25 up front. The writer is expecting that the price for MSFT will not go above $43.25 (The Strike Price of $42 plus the money collected of $1.25) between now and expiration. The writer is obligated to fulfill the contract if the buyer chooses, so anytime MSFT is above $42, the writer is obligated to sell those shares to the buyer at $42.00. If the price goes below $42, the buyer will not choose to exercise the option as the buyer can buy the shares for less than $42 in the open market.

In summary, the Buyer of a CALL option expects the stock price to go up, while the seller (writer) expects the price to go down.

PUT Options

A PUT Option gives the buyer the right to sell a stock at a set price (Strike Price) within a set time frame (until the Expiration).

Example: A PUT $42 MSFT APR $0.45. This is a contract that gives the buyer the right to sell MSFT at $42 per share (agreed upon Strike Price) by the 3rd Friday in April (Expiration Date).

In the above example, MSFT is trading at $42.80 and there are 28 days until expiration. So, why would someone sell the right to sell MSFT shares at $42.00 when MSFT is trading at $42.80? Well, the $0.45 that it would cost the buyer is the option price, and that goes to the seller (or what is referred to as the Writer - as they are WRITING the contract). In this case, the writer is willing to sell a contract and collect the $0.45 up front. The writer is expecting that the price for MSFT will not go below $41.55 (The Strike Price of $42 less the money collected of $0.45) between now and expiration. The writer is obligated to fulfill the contract if the buyer chooses, so anytime MSFT is below $42, the writer is obligated to buy those shares from the buyer at $42.00. If the price goes above $42, the buyer will not choose to exercise the option as the buyer can sell the shares for more than $42 in the open market.

In summary, the Buyer of a PUT option expects the stock price to go down, while the seller (writer) expects the price to go up.

Traded like stocks....

Option contracts are traded like stocks. This means that there is no set "selling" price, but the price is determined by the market. The market refers to buyers and sellers who come together to exchange their holdings for cash. When more buyers come to the market, it pushes prices up as the buyers have to bid higher in order to entice sellers. And if more sellers come to the market, they have to offer lower prices to entice buyers to buy their holdings.

Example: If you own a car dealership, and you have 100 BMW's on your lot, and a BMW normal sells for $70,000. If your normal inventory is 50 vehicles, it will be hard to sell all 100 BMW's you currently have. So, you would lower the price some to attract more buyers.

Now, if you have only 20 vehicles, you don't want to be out of inventory and you want to make the best profit you can, so you won't sell any vehicles for less than $70,000 and will probably raise the prices even higher.

So, when you hear the phrase "The market determines the price", it is referring to the dynamics between buyers and sellers. These dynamics are constantly changing, that is why prices move constantly during the day.

Option Prices, continued...

While Option Prices are determined by the market, there are still some variables that determine what that option price should be. These include:

>Where the stock price is in relation to the Strike Price
>How much time is left before expiration
>How volatile are the stock markets
>How volatile is the individual stock for the option you have

All of these factor into what traders feel is the appropriate price for an option. The action between these traders is what results in the "Market Price". Sometimes, the market prices will get out of line, or become too different from what the prices should be. During these times, traders will take advantage of that discrepancy until the market prices gets back to where they should be.

Relation to Stock Price.....

One of the components of an Option Contract is the Strike Price. This is the agreed upon price per the contract. For a CALL Contract this is the agreed upon price that the buyer can purchase shares at. For a PUT Contract, this is the agreed upon price that the buyer can sell shares at.

Example: MSFT CALL APR $40 allows the buyer to purchase MSFT shares at $40 anytime between the purchase of the option and expiration. MSFT PUT APR $40 allows the buyer to sell MSFT shares at $40 anytime between the purchase of the option and expiration.

The $40 is called the Strike Price. There are many different Strike Prices offered, so choosing one becomes an important part of trading options (more on that in a later blog). But the relationship between the Strike Price and the Stock Price helps drive the change in the option value.

Example: If MSFT was trading at $41.46, and you purchased a MSFT CALL APR $40 for $2.16, then if the price moves of MSFT goes up, the value of the CALL Option goes up.

Impact of Stock Price increase on CALL Option Prices.

	Day 0	Day 1	% Chg
Stock Price	41.46	42.00	1.3%
Option Price			
Call APR $40	2.16	2.57	19.0%
Call APR $41	1.08	1.37	26.9%
Call APR $42	0.59	0.73	23.7%

You can see from the table how a relatively small move in the stock price can have a large impact on the option price. If you had purchased the CALL APR $41 for $1.08, you would be able to sell that option the next day for $1.35. However, just as the price of your option can move higher quickly, it can go down just as quickly.

Impact of Stock Price decrease on CALL Option Prices.

	Day 0	Day 1	% Chg
Stock Price	41.46	41.00	-1.1%
Option Price			
Call APR $40	2.16	1.82	-15.7%
Call APR $41	1.08	0.85	-21.3%
Call APR $42	0.59	0.48	-18.6%

Again, you can see how a relatively small change in the stock price has an outsized impact on the Option Price.

PUT Option Pricing

The mechanics for PUT options are the same for CALL options (how they trade, how their value is determined, significance of how close to the Strike Price the Stock Price is, etc....). However, the major difference in that with a PUT option you are locking in a SELLING price for shares vs. a BUYING price for shares.

Simple Reminder: When you BUY PUTS, you want the Stock Price to go DOWN. As the Stock Price goes DOWN, the value of your PUT Option goes UP!

The reason for this is that with the PUT contract you have locked in a selling price (Strike Price). So, if you buy a MSFT PUT APR $42, you have purchased the right to sell shares at $42. If the stock price for MSFT goes lower, your contract becomes more valuable.

Example: You purchase MSFT PUT APR $42 when MSFT was trading at $41.46, and you paid $1.03 for the Option. Now, MSFT drops to $40. Your option gives you the right to sell shares at $42, even though you can only sell shares on the market for $40. So, you have a $2 value in your contract. And that value will get bigger as the stock price goes lower.

Impact of Stock Price decrease on PUT Option Prices.

	Day 0	Day 1	% Chg
Stock Price	41.46	41.00	-1.1%
Option Price			
Put APR $40	0.30	0.42	40.0%
Put APR $41	0.57	0.80	40.4%
Put APR $42	1.03	1.38	34.0%

The ability to sell your shares at a set price (Strike Price) gains in value as the actual price (Stock Price) declines. That is the benefit of PUT Options.

Impact of Stock Price increase on PUT Option Prices.

	Day 0	Day 1	% Chg
Stock Price	41.46	42.00	1.3%
Option Price			
Put APR $40	0.30	0.17	-43.3%
Put APR $41	0.57	0.30	-47.4%
Put APR $42	1.03	0.63	-38.8%

Proximity to the stock price.....

When selecting a Strike Price to purchase, you must understand the relationship between the Stock Price and the Strike Price.

The Strike Price is the price that the Buyer and Seller are agreeing to trade shares for. With a CALL the buyer is locking in the purchase price. With a PUT the buyer is locking in a sales price.

Example: If Company XYZ is trading at $46.75 (Stock Price), and you were looking to purchase a CALL option, there are several strike prices you can choose from. You could choose a CALL $46 or a CALL $47 or even a CALL $50. In this scenario the $46 CALL would cost you more than the $47 and the $50, because it offers you the best value (ie. Buying at a lower price). The CALL $47 would cost more than the $50.

So, when looking at a CALL, the higher the Strike Price, the lower the Option Price.

For PUTS, the relationship is just reversed. Since the buyer is locking in a selling price, the higher the Strike Price the higher the Option Price. In the previous example, if you were buying PUTS, the $50 Strike would be the most costly, and the $46 the least costly.

The Money....... In, At and OUT

In, At and OUT of the Money are used to describe the relationship between the Stock Price and the Strike Price.

IN the Money – refers to options that have some real value to them already. For instance, if you are buying a call (will stay with the same example as above), and the Stock Price is $46.75, any Strike Price below that is IN the Money because if you were to exercise the option, and buy the stock at the agreed upon Strike Price, you could buy the stock cheaper than if you bought the stock in the open market. If you bought a CALL $46, you could buy the shares of XYZ company at $46.00 instead of the $46.75 in the open market. So, why wouldn't everyone do this... buy a CALL $46 and make the $0.75 difference. Well, because in order to purchase the CALL $46, it would cost you more than the $0.75. Depending on how much time is left in the option until expiration and how volatile the markets are, the Option Price could be substantially higher than the $0.75 spread.

AT the Money – refers to options whose Strike Price and Stock Price are very close. In the example we have been using, with the Stock Price of $46.75, a CALL $47 would be AT the Money.

OUT of the Money – refers to options that do not have any real value, yet. Using the same example from above, with the Stock Price at $46.75, the CALL $50 would be out of the money.

How to tell if an Option is IN, AT or OUT of the Money

An easy way to remember if an option is IN the money or not, ask yourself: Would you rather exercise your contract or go into the open market? If you would rather have the contract, then it is IN THE MONEY. For instance, you have a PUT$50, but the stock price is at $50.60, you would be OUT of the Money because you would rather sell your shares in the open market, than through the options contract.

Strike Price is…	CALL	PUT
Above the Stock Price	IN the Money	OUT of the Money
Near the Stock Price	AT the Money	AT the Money
Below the Stock Price	OUT of the Money	IN the Money

MSFT (MICROSOFT CORP) Options Chain

Dec 10, 2017 @ 10:02 ET

Exchange: Cboe Options Range: Near the Money Size: 4x10 Expiration: 2017 December [View Chain]

Bid: 84.16 Ask: 84.17 Vol: 24489106 Last 84.16 Change +1.67

Calls — DECEMBER 2017 (EXPIRATION: 12/08)

Strike	Last	Net	Bid	Ask	Vol	Int
MSFT1708L83.5-E	0.60	+0.51	0.58	0.72	227	1766
MSFT1708L84-E	0.12	+0.09	0.10	0.23	1236	2784
MSFT1708L84.5-E	0.01	-0.01	0.0	4.30	385	1513
MSFT1708L85-E	0.01	0.0	0.0	0.01	20	2518

Puts — DECEMBER 2017 (EXPIRATION: 12/08)

Strike	Last	Net	Bid	Ask	Vol	Int
MSFT1708X83.5-E	0.01	-0.98	0.0	4.30	147	1274
MSFT1708X84-E	0.03	-1.74	0.0	10.00	1843	5214
MSFT1708X84.5-E	0.47	-1.63	0.26	0.40	574	764
MSFT1708X85-E	0.92	-1.80	0.70	0.92	61	886

Calls — DECEMBER 2017 (EXPIRATION: 12/15)

Strike	Last	Net	Bid	Ask	Vol	Int
MSFT1715L83.5-E	1.12	+0.64	0.68	1.23	322	1864
MSFT1715L84-E	0.87	+0.55	0.76	1.27	251	8892
MSFT1715L84.5-E	0.57	+0.41	0.54	0.66	323	2751
MSFT1715L85-E	0.36	+0.24	0.29	0.46	1103	20524

Puts — DECEMBER 2017 (EXPIRATION: 12/15)

Strike	Last	Net	Bid	Ask	Vol	Int
MSFT1715X83.5-E	0.49	-1.15	0.03	0.54	111	1971
MSFT1715X84-E	0.63	-1.39	0.61	1.08	1010	7161
MSFT1715X84.5-E	0.91	-1.77	0.86	1.33	12	1959
MSFT1715X85-E	1.26	-1.60	1.15	1.24	56	8650

Calls — DECEMBER 2017 (EXPIRATION: 12/22)

Strike	Last	Net	Bid	Ask	Vol	Int
MSFT1722L83.5-E	1.23	+0.32	1.39	1.53	24	360
MSFT1722L84-E	1.16	+0.59	1.11	1.61	53	637

Puts — DECEMBER 2017 (EXPIRATION: 12/22)

Strike	Last	Net	Bid	Ask	Vol	Int
MSFT1722X83.5-E	0.75	-0.97	0.69	0.88	33	140
MSFT1722X84-E	0.97	-1.46	0.90	1.09	43	1070

Above is an example of Option Quotes from the website: http://www.cboe.com/delayedquote/quote-table

The above quote is for Microsoft (MSFT).

Last is the last price per share that the option contract was traded for.

Bid is the current highest price someone is willing to pay for a contract

Ask is the current lowest price someone is willing to sell a contract for

Vol is the number of contracts that have been traded during the latest trading session

Int is the total number of contracts that have been opened, but no yet closed.

Generally, when looking to trade options, your focus should be on the following:

Higher VOL and OPEN INTEREST. The more contracts that are traded, the better your options contract will reflect the true value of changes in the underlying stock. It also usually means that the option premium is lower, as well as the spread between Bid and Ask prices.

Time Frame – generally, the further out EXPIRATION is, the higher the option price. However, you want to give yourself some time for the price to move. We look to trade options contracts that don't expire for 4 to 6 weeks. If you are trending with the market, this gives you time to weather any fluctuations in that trend. Remember, not all prices move occur in a straight line.

Strike Price – we generally look for a STRIKE PRICE At the Money or just OUT of the Money. This is because we are close enough to the STOCK PRICE that we will see moves in the option price more quickly as the STOCK PRICE moves.

INPUT DATA SHEET

How do we use all this information we gather, first we have to gather, save and store the information, the best way we found was to set up an input sheet that we input the data daily. We then set up an excel macro to install the new data from the input sheet into the appropriate cells on the next several pages we can see an example of all the information we track daily. We don't want to spend too much time gathering information. We want to spend more time study the data, and then make a winning decision. We can find all this information on two sites, stock charts. com and the wall street journal data center both can be accessed for free on line. the input example on the next few pages provides, all the information needed to calculate the formulas for the Dow, S&P, Nasdaq, VIX, gold, world NDX and the market.

The example input sheet on the next pages provides three columns of information, first is the source column, providing the location of the data. The second column is the information column, and the last column is the data we gather daily. There are a few ways we gather this information qualitative analysis and direct data from the source. How we analyze our qualitative data is by charting the formulas and volume. The formulas that have an up or down data input are charted and then inputted as per the daily chart, if the chart is up the we input an up signal and visa versa. The volume is inputted three ways, high, medium, and low, this is also gathered by reviewing the daily chart information. The global, Asia pacific, Europe, Americas and other countries are gathered by simple counting the up and down countries for the day and then inputting the data accordingly. all other data is copied directly form the source

Source	Info	
WSJ	Date	6/1/2017
WSJ	Nasdaq	6,246.83
WSJ	S&P	2430.06
WSJ	DJIA	21,144.18
WSJ	VIX	10.09
WSJ	NASDAQ Adv Issue	2174
WSJ	NASDAQ Dec Issue	718
WSJ	NASDAQ Adv Vol	1481958570
WSJ	NASDAQ Dec Vol	448582900
WSJ	NASDAQ Arms Index	
WSJ	NYSE Adv Issue	2467
WSJ	NYSE Dec Issue	540
WSJ	NYSE Adv Vol	3,072,893,744
WSJ	NYSE Dec Vol	733,483,246
WSJ	NYSE Arms Index	
WSJ	CBOE Volatility	10.09
WSJ	NYSE New High Issues	401
WSJ	NYSE New Low Issues	132
WSJ	NASDAQ New High Issues	393
WSJ	NASDAQ New Low Issues	208
WSJ	Global - Issues Up	4
WSJ	Global - Issues Down	-
	Global - Issues yr Up	4
	Global - Issues yr Down	-
WSJ	Asia Pacific - Issues Up	16
WSJ	Asia Pacific - Issues Down	4
	Asia Pacific - Issues yrUp	19
	Asia Pacific - Issues yr Down	1
WSJ	Europe - Issues Up	22
WSJ	Europe - Issues Down	2
	Europe - Issues yr Up	23
	Europe - Issues yr Down	1

WSJ	Americas - Issues Up	6
WSJ	Americas - Issues Down	1
	Americas - Issues yr Up	7
	Americas - Issues yr Down	-
WSJ	Other Countries - Issues Up	2
WSJ	Other Countries - Issues Down	1
	Other Countries - Issues yr Up	2
	Other Countries - Issues yr Down	1
Stock Charts	DJIA Accumulation/Distribution	up
Stock Charts	DJIA Parabolic SAR	20645.62
Stock Charts	DJIA Bollinger Bands High	21,201.05
Stock Charts	DJIA Bollinger Bands Low	20,692.23
Stock Charts	DJIA Volume	med
Stock Charts	DJIA Slow Stochastic - Up	
Stock Charts	DJIA Slow Stochastic - Down	1
Stock Charts	DJIA Pring Know Sure Thing - UP	
Stock Charts	DJIA Pring Know Sure Thing - Down	1
Stock Charts	DJIA Chaikin Money Flow - Up	1
Stock Charts	DJIA Chaikin Money Flow - Down	
	DJIA Money Flow - Up	1
	DJIA Money Flow - Down	
Stock Charts	DJIA Rate of Change - Up	1
Stock Charts	DJIA Rate of Change - Down	

WSJ	Americas - Issues Up	6
WSJ	Americas - Issues Down	1
	Americas - Issues yr Up	7
	Americas - Issues yr Down	-
WSJ	Other Countries - Issues Up	2
WSJ	Other Countries - Issues Down	1
	Other Countries - Issues yr Up	2
	Other Countries - Issues yr Down	1
Stock Charts	DJIA Accumulation/Distribution	up
Stock Charts	DJIA Parabolic SAR	20645.62
Stock Charts	DJIA Bollinger Bands High	21,201.05
Stock Charts	DJIA Bollinger Bands Low	20,692.23
Stock Charts	DJIA Volume	med
Stock Charts	DJIA Slow Stochastic - Up	
Stock Charts	DJIA Slow Stochastic - Down	1
Stock Charts	DJIA Pring Know Sure Thing - UP	
Stock Charts	DJIA Pring Know Sure Thing - Down	1
Stock Charts	DJIA Chaikin Money Flow - Up	1
Stock Charts	DJIA Chaikin Money Flow - Down	
	DJIA Money Flow - Up	**1**

Stock Charts	S&P Money Flow - Down	
Stock Charts	S&P Rate of Change - Up	1
Stock Charts	S&P Rate of Change - Down	
Stock Charts	S&P Average Directional Movement - Up	2
Stock Charts	S&P Average Directional Movement - Down	
Stock Charts	S&P True Strength Index - Up	1
Stock Charts	S&P True Strength Index - down	
Stock Charts	S&P CCI - UP	1
Stock Charts	S&P CCI - Down	
Stock Charts	S&P PMO - UP	1
Stock Charts	S&P PMO - Down	
Stock Charts	S&P Pivot Location	pr1
Stock Charts	S&P Pivot - Up	1
Stock Charts	S&P Pivot - Down	
Stock Charts	NASDAQ Accumulation/Distribution	up
Stock Charts	NASDAQ Parabolic SAR	6,256.64
Stock Charts	NASDAQ Bollinger Bands High	6,250.62
Stock Charts	NASDAQ Bollinger Bands Low	6,022.84
Stock Charts	NASDAQ Volume	med
Stock Charts	NASDAQ Slow Stochastic - Up	1
Stock Charts	NASDAQ Slow Stochastic - Down	
Stock Charts	NASDAQ Pring Know Sure Thing - UP	
Stock Charts	NASDAQ Pring Know Sure Thing - Down	1

Stock Charts	NASDAQ Chaikin Money Flow - Up	1
Stock Charts	NASDAQ Chaikin Money Flow - Down	
Stock Charts	NASDAQ Money Flow - Up	1
Stock Charts	NASDAQ Money Flow - Down	
Stock Charts	NASDAQ Rate of Change - Up	1
Stock Charts	NASDAQ Rate of Change - Down	
Stock Charts	NASDAQ Average Directional Movement - Up	1
Stock Charts	NASDAQ Average Directional Movement - Down	1
Stock Charts	NASDAQ True Strength Index - Up	1
Stock Charts	NASDAQ True Strength Index - Down	
Stock Charts	NASDAQ CCI - UP	1
Stock Charts	NASDAQ CCI - Down	
Stock Charts	NASDAQ PMO - UP	1
Stock Charts	NASDAQ PMO - Down	
Stock Charts	NASDAQ Pivot Location	pr1
Stock Charts	NASDAQ Pivot - Up	1
Stock Charts	NASDAQ Pivot - Down	
Stock Charts	NDX - Close	5,816.51
Stock Charts	NDX - Bollinger Bands High	5,828.10
Stock Charts	NDX - Bollinger Bands Low	5,575.86

Stock Charts	VIX Fast Stochastic - Up	
Stock Charts	VIX Fast Stochastic - Down	1
Stock Charts	VIX Pring Know Sure Thing - UP	1
Stock Charts	VIX Pring Know Sure Thing - Down	
Stock Charts	VIX Rate of Change - Up	
Stock Charts	VIX Rate of Change - Down	1
Stock Charts	VIX Average Directional Movement - Up	
Stock Charts	VIX Average Directional Movement - Down	2
Stock Charts	VIX True Strength Index - Up	
Stock Charts	VIX True Strength Index - Down	1
Stock Charts	VIX CCI - UP	
Stock Charts	VIX CCI - Down	1
Stock Charts	VIX PMO - UP	
Stock Charts	VIX PMO - Down	1
Stock Charts	VIX Pivot Location	ps1
Stock Charts	VIX Pivot - Up	
Stock Charts	VIX Pivot - Down	1
Stock Charts	Gold Accumulation/Distribution	up
Stock Charts	Gold Parabolic SAR	1248.63
Stock Charts	Gold Bollinger Bands High	1282.42
Stock Charts	Gold Bollinger Bands Low	1208.25
Stock Charts	Gold Volume	low
Stock Charts	Gold Slow Stochastic - Up	1

Stock Charts	Gold Slow Stochastic - Down	
Stock Charts	Gold Pring Know Sure Thing - UP	1
Stock Charts	Gold Pring Know Sure Thing - Down	
Stock Charts	Gold Chaikin Money Flow - Up	1
Stock Charts	Gold Chaikin Money Flow - Down	
Stock Charts	Gold Money Flow - Up	
Stock Charts	Gold Money Flow - Down	1
Stock Charts	Gold Rate of Change - Up	
Stock Charts	Gold Rate of Change - Down	1
Stock Charts	Gold Average Directional Movement - Up	1
Stock Charts	Gold Average Directional Movement - Down	1
Stock Charts	Gold True Strength Index - Up	1
Stock Charts	Gold True Strength Index - Down	
Stock Charts	Gold CCI - UP	
Stock Charts	Gold CCI - Down	1
Stock Charts	Gold PMO - UP	1
Stock Charts	Gold PMO - Down	
Stock Charts	Gold Pivot Location	pr1
Stock Charts	Gold Pivot - Up	1
Stock Charts	Gold Pivot - Down	
Stock Charts	Gold - Close	1270.10

Summary Sheet

The Summary Sheet is our score card on how the markets are trending. By putting a percentage to each index and combining the results to formulate an indicator for the tread of the overall market. We calculate market trends and contra trend information. The market trend consists of six values, 1, the overall market, 2, is the world daily market, 3, Dow jones 4, S&P 500 5, Nasdaq and 6, NDX. For the contra signal we use two indexes, gold index and the VIX. We collect detailed information for each of the values listed previously and analyze various signals, determining whether the signal is bullish or bearish.

We will detail that analysis and have a bullish or bearish signal determined. The summary percentage below 40 (bearish) are highlighted in red. Percentages above 60 (bullish) are highlighted in green. Contra indicators are highlighted the same way however in bullish markets we want to see contra indicators as red. Knowing the trend of the market is key and we always want to invest on the same side as the primary trend of the market. Highlighting the highs and lows of the index, provides us with vital information. First it provides the total formula data at the time of the change. The market can turn on a dime or it can run in cycles by tracking the total up and down numbers, the convergence and divergence of the index and the percentages when the market change can provide helpful insight on buy points and sell points. The markets can trend in cycles and by tracking the past cycles, this information can provide helpful insight on the future cycles of the market.

Date	World Markets	Daily	Yearly	DOW	S&P	CONTRA VIX	Nasdaq	NDX	CONTRA Gold	Indicators Trends market	contra	Dow	Nasdaq	S&P	vix	gold
3/5/2018	75.0%	63.8%	27.6%	60.0%	45.0%	76.5%	80.0%	60.0%	80.0%	65%	78%	24,874.76	7,330.70	2,720.94	18.11	1,319.90
3/2/2018	37.5%	12.3%	30.4%	30.0%	45.0%	64.7%	75.0%	40.0%	65.0%	40%	65%	24,538.06	7,257.87	2,691.25	19.98	1,323.40
3/1/2018	12.5%	12.5%	30.4%	20.0%	30.0%	41.2%	45.0%	60.0%	90.0%	24%	66%	24,608.98	7,180.56	2,677.67	24.15	1,305.20
2/28/2018	25.0%	10.3%	51.7%	25.0%	40.0%	52.9%	40.0%	100.0%	70.0%	28%	61%	25,029.20	7,273.01	2,713.01	20.47	1,363.40
2/27/2018	62.5%	32.8%	58.6%	55.0%	70.0%	52.9%	70.0%	80.0%	95.0%	58%	74%	25,410.03	7,330.35	2,744.28	17.99	1,318.60
2/26/2018	87.5%	84.5%	56.9%	80.0%	75.0%	88.2%	90.0%	80.0%	50.0%	83%	69%	25,709.27	7,421.46	2,779.60	16.12	1,332.80
2/23/2018	75.0%	77.4%	51.6%	65.0%	70.0%	88.2%	85.0%	80.0%	70.0%	74%	79%	25,309.99	7,337.39	2,747.30	16.37	1,330.30
2/22/2018	37.5%	31.8%	48.3%	50.0%	35.0%	88.2%	50.0%	80.0%	70.0%	46%	79%	24,962.48	7,210.09	2,703.96	13.77	1,332.10
2/21/2018	62.5%	75.0%	48.3%	25.0%	45.0%	82.4%	40.0%	80.0%	70.0%	52%	76%	24,797.78	7,234.31	2,701.33	19.89	1,332.10
2/20/2018	62.5%	42.3%	39.3%	45.0%	35.0%	64.7%	50.0%	80.0%	65.0%	47%	57%	25,219.38	7,234.31	2,716.20	20.50	1,356.20
2/16/2018	62.5%	36.5%	36.2%	45.0%	40.0%	52.9%	40.0%	100.0%	65.0%	46%	59%	25,219.38	7,239.47	2,753.22	20.99	1,311.98
2/15/2018	87.5%	89.7%	44.8%	60.0%	55.0%	64.7%	65.0%	40.0%	35.0%	71%	50%	24,200.37	7,235.43	2,731.20	18.19	1,355.30
2/14/2018	100.0%	79.3%	36.2%	45.0%	40.0%	64.7%	60.0%	40.0%	35.0%	65%	50%	24,893.49	7,143.62	2,662.94	18.19	1,358.00
2/13/2018	87.5%	50.9%	22.4%	35.0%	40.0%	47.1%	40.0%	20.0%	50.0%	51%	49%	24,640.45	7,013.51	2,662.94	23.47	1,330.40
2/12/2018	62.5%	81.8%	19.0%	36.8%	45.0%	52.9%	40.0%	20.0%	65.0%	53%	59%	24,601.27	6,981.96	2,656.00	27.16	1,326.40
2/9/2018	62.5%	0.0%	0.0%	35.0%	40.0%	52.9%	35.0%	20.0%	85.0%	35%	69%	24,190.90	6,874.49	2,619.55	26.47	1,315.70
2/8/2018	25.0%	24.1%	24.1%	5.0%	20.0%	11.8%	15.0%	40.0%	80.0%	18%	46%	23,860.46	6,777.16	2,581.00	31.60	1,319.00
2/7/2018	62.5%	78.9%	44.6%	15.0%	25.0%	35.3%	15.0%	40.0%	95.0%	39%	65%	24,893.35	7,051.98	2,681.66	28.74	1,314.60
2/6/2018	62.5%	3.4%	60.3%	23.3%	15.0%	29.4%	10.0%	40.0%	70.0%	27%	55%	24,912.77	7,115.88	2,695.14	31.09	1,329.50
2/5/2018	37.5%	3.4%	60.3%	5.0%	10.0%	0.0%	5.0%	60.0%	80.0%	12%	40%	24,345.75	6,967.53	2,648.94	44.08	1,336.50
2/2/2018	50.0%	56.1%	82.8%	36.8%	15.0%	5.9%	5.0%	60.0%	80.0%	27%	43%	25,520.96	7,240.95	2,762.13	17.31	1,337.30
2/1/2018	50.0%	37.9%	87.5%	35.0%	40.0%	52.9%	35.0%	60.0%	40.0%	39%	38%	26,186.71	7,385.86	2,821.98	14.54	1,347.90
1/31/2018	62.5%	50.0%	87.9%	55.0%	40.0%	41.2%	30.0%	20.0%	55.0%	48%	48%	26,149.39	7,411.48	2,823.81	13.13	1,343.10
1/30/2018	25.0%	1.8%	89.5%	25.0%	30.0%	5.9%	35.0%	40.0%	60.0%	23%	33%	26,076.89	7,402.48	2,822.43	14.27	1,339.20
1/29/2018	50.0%	32.8%	93.1%	40.0%	50.0%	5.9%	55.0%	20.0%	60.0%	46%	33%	26,439.48	7,466.51	2,853.53	13.97	1,340.00
1/26/2018	62.5%	79.2%	91.1%	95.0%	85.0%	41.2%	90.0%	20.0%	15.0%	77%	28%	26,616.71	7,505.77	2,872.87	11.08	1,352.10
1/25/2018	37.5%	36.8%	89.7%	70.0%	60.0%	41.2%	55.0%	80.0%	5.0%	52%	23%	26,392.79	7,411.16	2,839.25	11.06	1,362.90
1/24/2018	87.5%	84.5%	93.1%	60.0%	65.0%	41.2%	80.0%	60.0%	35.0%	75%	38%	26,210.81	7,460.29	2,839.13	11.06	1,336.70
1/23/2018	75.0%	81.4%	93.1%	89.5%	75.0%	35.3%	95.0%	60.0%	25.0%	78%	30%	26,214.60	7,408.03	2,832.97	10.92	1,331.90
1/22/2018	75.0%	79.3%	93.1%	75.0%	60.0%	35.3%	95.0%	60.0%	45.0%	85%	40%	26,071.72	7,336.38	2,810.30	11.46	1,333.10
1/19/2018	37.5%	86.0%	89.7%	85.0%	75.0%	35.3%	85.0%	80.0%	20.0%	72%	28%	26,017.81	7,296.05	2,798.05	12.22	1,327.20
1/18/2018	50.0%	48.3%	89.7%	85.0%	80.0%	17.6%	60.0%	80.0%	55.0%	58%	36%	26,115.65	7,298.28	2,802.56	11.96	1,329.20
1/17/2018	50.0%	56.9%	94.8%	65.0%	80.0%	41.2%	70.0%	60.0%	30.0%	70%	18%	25,792.86	7,223.69	2,776.42	11.91	1,337.10
1/16/2018	50.0%	63.2%	94.8%	65.0%	65.0%	5.9%	50.0%	60.0%	25.0%	63%	15%	25,803.19	7,261.06	2,786.24	11.31	1,334.90
1/12/2018	50.0%	77.2%	94.8%	95.0%	90.0%	29.4%	95.0%	80.0%	5.0%	81%	17%	25,747.73	7,211.78	2,786.24	11.78	1,334.90
1/11/2018	62.5%	59.6%	94.8%	85.0%	85.0%	47.1%	95.0%	80.0%	30.0%	80%	47%	25,574.73	7,211.78	2,711.78	9.71	1,322.50
1/10/2018	62.5%	29.3%	96.6%	55.0%	55.0%	47.1%	60.0%	100.0%	35.0%	52%	41%	25,369.13	7,153.57	2,748.23	9.71	1,319.30
1/9/2018	50.0%	77.2%	98.2%	70.0%	70.0%	41.2%	80.0%	80.0%	40.0%	72%	43%	25,385.80	7,163.58	2,751.29	10.40	1,313.70
1/8/2018	87.5%	82.1%	100.0%	70.0%	85.0%	52.9%	80.0%	80.0%	25.0%	81%	36%	25,283.00	7,157.39	2,747.71	9.42	1,320.40
1/5/2018	75.0%	93.0%	98.3%	85.0%	80.0%	47.1%	85.0%	80.0%	80.0%	84%	43%	25,295.57	7,136.56	2,743.15	9.77	1,322.30
1/4/2018	87.5%	91.4%	98.3%	75.0%	80.0%	52.9%	80.0%	100.0%	25.0%	83%	42%	25,075.13	7,077.91	2,732.99	9.16	1,321.60
1/3/2018	87.5%	87.3%	94.8%	70.0%	80.0%	70.6%	85.0%	60.0%	25.0%	82%	48%	24,922.68	7,065.53	2,713.06	9.00	1,318.50
1/2/2018	75.0%	67.3%	75.9%	45.0%	55.0%	58.8%	75.0%	40.0%	10.0%	63%	34%	24,824.01	7,005.90	2,695.81	9.47	1,316.10

S&P Formula Spreadsheet

The S&P Formula spreadsheet is where all the information we gather and install on our input data sheet, is installed specifically for the S&P information. First The green and red line across the page running through the formulas represents the market hitting its highs and lows for the trend. Installing highs and lows provide useful information. For example, we can see at a glance where the total calculations of the formulas work as the market changes, it also provides information on the formulas strengths and weakness as the market changes either bullish or bearish.

The c/d column is the convergence and divergence of the total up and the total down calculation of the signals from the various formulas, positive numbers represent a strengthening condition. One of the keys to any formula is understanding the numbers, the S&P formula spreadsheet on the next page shows two market highs and one market low in the time frame on this snap shot 3/7/18 to 4/25/18. On 3/9/18 we have the S&P hitting a high of 2786.57 our formula is showing 16 up signals and 4 down signals with a 80% confirmation ratio and a plus 12 (c/d) convergence / divergence ratio. We consider this a strong signal that the market will change in direction as it did. Looking at 3/9/18 to 4/2/18 we can see the (c/d) convergence / divergence column changing from green to red as the market declines and the up% column drops to confirm the direction of the move. On 4/2/18 the S&P hit the low of the trend 2581.12 with 2 up signals and 18 down signals with the up % at 15% and the (c/d) convergence/ divergence at (-16) we considered this a strong signal that the market will change in direction, as it did for the next 16 days to 4/18/18 when it hit the high of the trend 2708.64 a 127.52 move up. Our last signal on 4/18/18, the total up signal 13 and total down signal is 7 the (c/d) convergence/ divergence is 6 and the up% is 65% We consider this a weak signal. Although the market is declining we are not receiving strong signals that can confirm the direction of the move. In this case we continue to track the data until we receive a stronger signal. we are looking for at least an 80% signal before we consider the move to be strong and a possible reversal in sight.

On the next page we are also displaying the (RSI) Relative Strength Index, trend, accumulation /distribution, parabolic Sar. The trend of the issue is very important we get this information from the Relative Strength Index, the 9day provides short term signals and the 14 provides a more smoothed signal either bullish or bearish. The chart also provides accumulation and distribution signal we simple do this by seeing if the issue or market is being accumulated then the day before. When the market is being accumulated more then the day before we install an up signal and if not, we install a down signal, accumulation and distribution is a key formula to watch.

The chart also provides the parabolic Sar the parabolic Sar has an up and down column to provide the direction of the Sar but the twist we put on the formula is installing a convergence/ divergence column. The convergence /divergence provide the strength of the formula, so if the formula is bullish or bearish we can see what direction the formula is provided. For example, on 3/9/18 the Sar is providing an up signal but the (c/d) is falling as is the market, on 4/2/18 the market hits the low of the trend the Sar is bearish (red) but the (c/d) column is rising as is the market.

Tech Smart

CLOSE	total up	total down	c/d	up %	0	NEGATIVE	Sum of Up	Sum of Down	RSI	Sum of Up	Sum of Down	RSI	Market - 9 Day RSI	up	down	TREND	up	down	Accum Dist	up	down	parabolic sar	c/d	up	down
2639.4	9	11	-2	45%	4.84	0.00	57.33	81.92	41.1706	131.53	154.97	45.9092	Bull	1	0	Bear	0	1	up	1	0	2,717.49	78.09	0	0
2634.56	7	13	-6	35%	35.73	0.00	74.29	81.92	47.5578	144.84	154.97	48.3106	Bull	1	0	Bear	0	1	down	0	1	2,612.29	22.27	0	0
2670.29	8	12	-4	40%	0.15	0.00	74.29	60.87	54.9645	175.08	119.24	59.4863	Bull	1	0	Bear	0	1	down	0	1	2,603.14	67.15	1	0
2670.14	10	10	-1	47%	22.98	0.00	117.85	60.87	65.9411	208.26	119.24	63.5908	Bull	1	0	Bear	0	1	down	0	1	2,593.20	76.94	1	0
2693.13	9	11	-6	45%	15.51	0.00	126.54	37.88	76.9614	208.26	156.00	57.1734	Bull	1	0	Bear	0	1	down	0	1	2,582.39	110.74	1	0
2708.64	13	7	6	65%	2.25	0.00	126.54	80.74	61.0479	243.13	203.49	54.4730	Bull	1	0	Bear	0	1	down	0	1	2,571.63	136.96	0	0
2706.39	17	3	14	85%	28.55	0.00	142.44	80.74	63.8229	241.38	148.11	62.0221	Bull	1	0	Bear	0	1	down	0	1	2,561.54	144.85	1	1
2677.84	16	4	12	80%	21.54	0.00	144.13	80.74	64.0948	213.33	194.04	52.3676	Bull	1	0	Bear	0	1	down	0	1	2,556.33	121.51	1	1
2656.3	14	6	8	70%	7.89	0.00	155.92	80.74	65.8835	262.08	194.04	57.4586	Bull	1	0	Bear	0	1	down	0	1	2,553.80	102.5	1	1
2663.59	14	6	8	70%	21.80	0.00	155.92	132.80	54.0039	262.08	241.78	52.0144	Bull	1	0	Bear	0	1	up	1	0	2,679.13	15.14	0	1
2642.19	10	10	0	50%	14.68	0.00	169.99	132.80	56.1412	240.28	310.02	43.6635	Bear	0	1	Bear	0	1	down	0	1	2,687.13	-44.94	1	1
2556.87	13	7	6	65%	43.71	0.00	169.99	125.74	57.4815	240.28	300.35	44.4444	Bear	0	1	Bear	0	1	up	1	0	2,595.70	61.17	1	0
2613.16	6	14	-8	27%	8.69	58.37	126.28	171.67	42.3830	200.59	300.35	40.0427	Bear	0	1	Bear	0	1	down	0	1	2,704.69	-91.53	1	0
2604.47	4	16	-12	20%			187.88	171.67	52.2542	191.90	339.44	36.1162	Bear	0	1	Bear	0	1	up	1	0	2,714.33	-109.86	0	1
2662.84	13	7	6	65%	18.15	0.00	187.88	168.73	52.6850	196.58	281.07	41.1557	Bear	0	1	Bear	0	1	up	1	0	2,724.57	-61.73	0	1
2644.69	14	6	8	70%	30.24	0.00	169.73	236.97	41.7335	178.43	283.22	38.6505	Bear	0	1	Bear	0	1	up	1	0	2,735.47	-90.78	1	1
2614.45	12	8	4	60%	33.33	0.00	139.49	241.98	36.5664	148.19	299.05	33.1343	Bear	0	1	Bear	0	1	up	1	0	2,747.07	-132.62	0	1
2551.12	2	18	-16	10%		39.73	110.18	241.98	31.2869	112.86	310.76	26.6214	Bear	0	1	Bear	0	1	up	1	0	2,758.40	-128.28	0	1
2640.87	11	9	2	55%	35.87		110.18	221.32	33.2368	114.86	260.56	30.5951	Bear	0	1	Bull	1	0	down	0	1	2,766.63	-125.76	0	0
2605	15	5	10	85%		0.62	78.99	221.32	26.3028	126.59	260.56	32.6979	Bear	0	1	Bull	1	0	down	0	1	2,775.00	-170	0	1
2612.62	15	5	10	85%		45.93	78.99	215.85	26.7908	138.76	253.94	35.4251	Bear	0	1	Bull	1	0	down	0	1	2,782.01	-169.39	0	0
2658.55	12	8	4	40%	70.29	0.00	78.99	185.75	29.8368	138.76	208.33	39.9781	Bear	0	1	Bull	1	0	down	0	1	2,790.18	-131.63	1	0
2588.16	1	19	-18	5%	55.43		8.70	203.46	4.1007	75.65	208.33	26.6392	Bear	0	1	Bull	1	0	down	0	1	2,798.69	-210.53	1	1
2643.69	3	17	-14	15%	68.24		8.70	151.58	5.4280	75.65	152.90	33.1000	Bear	0	1	Bull	1	0	down	0	1	2,801.90	-158.21	1	1
2711.93	9	11	-6	35%	5.01		56.30	83.34	40.3180	105.34	84.66	55.4421	Bull	1	0	Bull	1	0	down	0	1	2,694.59	17.34	0	0
2716.94	8	12	-4	40%	4.02	0.00	68.47	78.33	46.6417	118.92	79.65	59.8882	Bull	1	0	Bull	1	0	down	0	1	2,694.59	22.35	0	0
2712.92	7	13	-4	35%	39.09		64.45	79.65	44.7259	114.90	114.99	49.9804	Bull	1	0	Bull	1	0	down	0	1	2,687.97	24.95	0	0
2752.01	12	8	4	60%	4.68		71.63	40.56	63.8470	114.90	107.17	51.7404	Bull	1	0	Bull	1	0	down	0	1	2,680.70	71.31	0	0
2747.33	8	12	-4	40%	2.15		66.95	40.56	62.2733	114.90	110.22	43.6152	Bull	1	0	Bull	1	0	down	0	1	2,672.97	74.36	0	0
2749.48	8	12	-4	40%	15.83		96.64	38.41	71.5587	142.52	140.34	50.3853	Bull	1	0	Bull	1	0	down	0	1	2,664.74	84.74	0	0
2765.31	11	9	2	55%	17.71		110.22	22.58	82.9970	185.86	124.51	59.8834	Bull	1	0	Bull	1	0	down	0	1	2,655.98	109.33	0	0
2783.02	13	7	6	65%	3.55		110.22	40.71	73.2700	188.46	106.80	63.8322	Bull	1	0	Bull	1	0	down	0	1	2,650.10	132.92	1	1
2786.57	17	3	14	75%	47.60	0.00	110.22	67.93	61.8693	188.49	118.12	61.4755	Bull	1	0	Bull	1	0	up	1	0	2,647.12	138.25	0	0
2738.97	15	5	10	75%	12.17		62.62	103.25	37.7525	140.89	134.14	51.2271	Bull	1	0	Bull	1	0	up	1	0	2,778.14	-39.17	1	1
2726.8	8	12	-4	40%		1.32	82.75	103.25	44.4892	129.74	134.14	49.1663	Bear	0	1	Bull	1	0	up	1	0	2,780.81	-54.01	1	1

S&P Formula Spreadsheet

The chart on the next page provides the close, totals, up/ down signals, (c/d) and up percentages, Bollinger bands and volume. first the Bollinger bands numbers, the signal is the c/d column as in most of our formulas, we like to install this feature when ever we can to provide a more precise direction of the formula. First looking at the Bollinger band formula the (c/d) column is the trigger when the (c/d) is trending lower the market is declining and when the (c/d) column is rising the market is rising. On 3/9/18 the (c/d) is at its low of -134.62 as the S&P hits its high of the trend 2786.57. On 4/2/2018 the S&P hit the low of the trend as the Bollinger band formula hit the low - 725.18 and then increased as the S&P ascended. On 4/18/18 the market top and the C/D top occurred simultaneously. Next on the chart is a volume column we install three words high med or low, we check the volume chart for the day and determine the level from the previous day.

Tech Smart

DATE	CLOSE	total up	total down	c/d	up %	bollanger bands high	low	bb c/d	high minus close	close minus low	high low close c/d	c/d bb minus c/d	bb/cd- (high-close+l c/d)	(close-low+h/clo se c/d)-bb c/d	c/d	up	down	volume	up	down
4/25/2018	2639.4	9	11	-2	45%	2716.28	2,582.43	133.85	76.88	56.97	-19.91	153.76	76.88	-96.79	-173.67	1	0	med	1	0
4/24/2018	2634.56	7	13	-6	35%	2716.73	2,579.30	137.43	82.17	55.26	-26.91	164.34	82.17	-109.08	-191.25	0	1	med	0	1
4/23/2018	2670.29	8	12	-4	40%	2717.78	2,580.65	137.13	47.49	89.64	42.15	94.98	47.49	-5.34	-52.83	0	1	med	1	0
4/20/2018	2670.14	9	10	-1	47%	2717.84	2,572.39	145.45	47.70	97.75	50.05	95.4	47.7	2.35	-45.35	0	1	high	0	1
4/19/2018	2693.13	9	11	-2	45%	2715.6	2,547.98	167.62	22.47	145.15	122.68	44.94	22.47	100.21	77.74	1	0	med	1	0
4/18/2018	2708.64	13	7	6	65%	2719.53	2,569.93	149.60	10.89	138.71	127.82	21.78	10.89	116.93	106.04	1	0	med	1	0
4/17/2018	2706.39	17	3	14	85%	2721.44	2,568.86	152.58	15.05	137.53	122.48	30.1	15.05	107.43	92.38	1	0	med	1	0
4/16/2018	2677.84	16	4	12	80%	2722.86	2,568.09	154.77	45.02	109.75	64.73	90.04	45.02	19.71	-25.31	1	0	med	1	0
4/13/2018	2656.3	14	6	8	70%	2728.59	2,559.77	168.82	72.29	96.53	24.24	144.58	72.29	-48.05	-120.34	1	0	med	1	0
4/12/2018	2663.99	14	6	8	70%	2752.87	2,554.60	198.27	88.88	109.39	20.51	177.76	88.88	-68.37	-157.25	1	0	med	1	0
4/11/2018	2642.19	10	10	0	50%	2765.56	2,550.46	215.10	123.37	91.73	-31.64	246.74	123.37	-155.01	-278.38	0	1	low	0	1
4/10/2018	2656.87	13	7	6	65%	2781.07	2,547.25	233.82	124.20	109.62	-14.58	248.4	124.2	-138.78	-262.98	1	0	med	1	0
4/9/2018	2613.16	6	14	-8	30%	2798.23	2,542.71	255.52	185.00	70.45	-114.62	370.14	185.00	-299.69	-484.76	0	1	low	0	1
4/6/2018	2604.47	4	16	-12	20%	2813.54	2,544.75	268.79	209.07	59.72	-149.35	418.14	209.07	-358.42	-567.49	0	1	med	1	0
4/5/2018	2662.84	13	7	6	65%	2818.08	2,553.65	264.43	155.24	109.19	-46.05	310.48	155.24	-201.29	-356.53	1	0	med	1	0
4/4/2018	2644.69	14	6	8	70%	2821.99	2,556.14	265.85	177.30	88.55	-88.75	354.6	177.3	-266.05	-443.35	1	0	med	1	0
4/3/2018	2614.45	12	8	4	60%	2826.57	2,560.91	265.66	211.12	53.54	-157.58	422.24	211.12	-368.70	-579.82	0	1	med	1	0
4/2/2018	2581.12	2	18	-16	10%	2826.27	2,570.85	255.42	245.15	10.27	-234.88	490.3	245.15	-480.03	-725.18	0	1	med	0	1
3/29/2018	2640.87	11	9	2	55%	2820.12	2,587.93	232.19	179.25	52.94	-126.31	358.5	179.25	-305.56	-484.81	1	0	med	1	0
3/28/2018	2605	5	15	-10	25%	2818.35	2,593.45	224.90	213.35	11.55	-201.80	426.7	213.35	-415.15	-628.50	0	1	med	0	1
3/27/2018	2612.62	5	15	-10	25%	2814.58	2,608.04	206.54	201.96	4.58	-197.38	403.92	201.96	-399.34	-601.30	0	1	med	1	0
3/26/2018	2658.55	8	12	-4	40%	2811.5	2,624.29	187.21	152.95	34.26	-118.69	305.9	152.95	-271.64	-424.59	1	0	med	1	0
3/23/2018	2588.26	1	19	-18	5%	2817.07	2,630.82	186.25	228.81	-42.56	-271.37	457.62	228.81	-500.18	-728.99	0	1	med	0	1
3/22/2018	2643.69	3	17	-14	15%	2801.51	2,662.29	139.22	157.82	-18.60	-176.42	315.64	157.82	-334.24	-492.06	0	1	med	1	0
3/21/2018	2711.93	7	13	-6	35%	2793.3	2,694.59	98.71	81.37	17.34	-64.03	162.74	81.37	-145.40	-226.77	0	1	med	1	0
3/20/2018	2716.94	8	12	-4	40%	2793.22	2,676.94	116.28	76.28	40.00	-36.28	152.56	76.28	-112.56	-188.84	1	0	med	1	0
3/19/2018	2712.92	7	13	-6	35%	2793.79	2,674.91	118.88	80.87	38.01	-42.86	161.74	80.87	-123.73	-204.60	1	0	med	1	0
3/16/2018	2752.01	12	8	4	60%	2793.95	2,676.67	117.28	41.94	75.34	33.40	83.88	41.94	-8.54	-50.48	1	0	high	1	0
3/15/2018	2747.33	8	12	-4	40%	2792.43	2,676.12	116.31	45.10	71.21	26.11	90.2	45.1	-18.99	-64.09	0	1	med	1	0
3/14/2018	2749.48	8	12	-4	40%	2791.65	2,672.02	119.63	42.17	77.46	35.29	84.34	42.17	-6.88	-49.05	0	1	med	1	0
3/13/2018	2765.31	11	9	2	55%	2793.77	2,661.25	132.52	28.46	104.06	75.60	56.92	28.46	47.14	18.68	0	1	med	1	0
3/12/2018	2783.02	13	7	6	65%	2792.81	2,651.28	141.53	9.79	131.74	121.95	19.58	9.79	112.16	102.37	1	0	med	1	0
3/9/2018	2786.57	17	3	14	85%	2791.96	2,635.78	156.18	5.39	150.79	145.40	10.78	5.39	140.01	134.62	1	0	med	1	0
3/8/2018	2738.97	15	5	10	75%	2793.87	2,613.32	180.55	54.90	125.65	70.75	109.8	54.9	15.85	-39.05	1	0	med	1	0
3/7/2018	2726.8	8	12	-4	40%	2789.96	2,611.50	178.46	63.16	115.30	52.14	126.32	63.16	-11.02	-74.18	0	1	med	0	1

S&P Formula Spreadsheet

The chart on the next page has a few formulas first the moving averages as you can see we have the 5,9,20,50,100,200 day moving averages. In the green and red column, we have the moving averages in conjunction with the close and other moving averages to give perspective and gauge the, strength of the move. The first few columns close /5 close /9 close/20 reflect the close of the day and the moving average of the close over the 5,9,20, days as per the column. The next several columns are moving averages in conjunction with other moving averages. The 5-day moving average with the 20-day moving average, also we have the 9/20, 20/50, 50,100,100,200.

When the moving average is higher than the close this is a red signal or (bearish) and when the moving average is lower than the close this is a bullish signal (green). Looking at the chart on the next page on 3/9/18 we see the S&P at the high of the trend as all the short-term signal are up, as the index drops the moving averages drop and turn red two days after the high of the trend. The market hit a low on 4/2/18 as you can see the moving averages are all in red except the long-term signals 50/100 and 100/200 day one of the best things about using moving averages as you can see it will keep you on the right side of the market either bullish or bearish.

The next four formulas on the chart on the next page are slow stochastic, Pring know sure thing, Chaikin money flow, and money flow. The slow stochastic and money flow are two formulas that are faster moving formulas then the Chaikin money flow, and the Prings know sure thing. In fast moving swings the slow stochastic and the money flow would be a good signal to watch but we need the slower moving signals like the Prings know sure thing and the Chaikin money flow to round out our perfect storm formula.

Tech Smart

S&P Formula Spreadsheet

The next section we have displayed is the MACD with a little twist. The MACD trigger is the 9-day moving average of the MACD, we installed a convergence/divergence column to highlight the difference between the MACD and the 9 day. When we set up a convergence / divergence column it reveals the movement of the formulas strength much clearer. By following the numbers rise and fall in the convergence / divergence column, we get a signal for market change. When the numbers change in direction in most cases so does the market. The next column is the average directional movement, we pull two signals from this formula we follow the ADX and the plus ADX signal if the ADX is moving up that is a up signal and if it is moving down it is a down signal and the same goes for the plus ADX signal, so this formula provides two numbers for this formula. the next two signals are fast moving signals the CCI commodity channel index and the PMO price momentum oscillator, we simply follow the direction of the movement of the formula if the formula is moving up then we install an up signal and if the formulas are moving down we install a down signal.

DATE	CLOSE	total up	total down	c/d	up %	rate of change	up	down	15%	85%	12 DAY	7.50%	92.50%	26 DAY	MACD	9 DAY	macd 9day convergence divergence
4/25/2019	2926.17	11	9	2	55%			1	438.9255	2461.429	2900.35	219.4628	2651.406	2870.87	-29.49	(26.69)	2.80
4/24/2019	2927.25	10	10	0	50%			1	439.0875	2456.711	2895.80	219.5438	2646.842	2866.39	-29.41	(25.50)	3.91
4/23/2019	2933.68	17	3	14	85%		1		440.052	2450.197	2890.25	220.026	2641.424	2861.45	-28.80	(24.04)	4.76
4/22/2019	2907.97	10	10	0	50%			1	436.1955	2446.389	2882.58	218.0978	2637.496	2855.59	-26.99	(22.24)	4.75
4/18/2019	2905.03	10	10	0	50%			1	435.7545	2442.35	2878.10	217.8773	2633.47	2851.35	-26.76	(22.49)	4.27
4/17/2019	2900.45	7	13	-6	35%			1	435.0675	2438.285	2873.35	217.5338	2629.461	2846.99	-26.36	(22.61)	3.75
4/16/2019	2907.06	12	8	4	60%		1		436.059	2432.512	2868.57	218.0295	2624.631	2842.66	-25.91	(22.57)	3.34
4/15/2019	2905.58	10	10	0	50%			1	435.837	2425.942	2861.78	217.9185	2619.52	2837.44	-24.34	(22.41)	1.93
4/12/2019	2907.41	15	5	10	75%		1		436.1115	2417.938	2854.05	218.0558	2613.858	2831.91	-22.14	(22.25)	-0.12
4/11/2019	2888.32	11	9	2	55%			1	433.248	2411.385	2854.05	216.624	2609.168	2825.79	-18.84	(22.13)	-3.29
4/10/2019	2888.21	12	8	4	60%		1		433.2315	2403.691	2836.92	216.6158	2604.107	2820.72	-16.20	(22.10)	-5.90
4/9/2019	2664.76	6	14	-8	30%			1	399.714	2428.158	2827.87	199.857	2615.394	2815.25	-12.62	(22.30)	-9.68
4/8/2019	2895.77	13	7	6	65%			1	434.3655	2422.291	2856.66	217.1828	2610.27	2827.45	-29.20	(23.02)	6.19
4/5/2019	2892.74	18	2	16	90%		1		433.911	2415.843	2849.75	216.9555	2604.958	2821.91	-27.84	(22.11)	5.73
4/4/2019	2879.78	14	6	8	70%			1	431.967	2410.202	2842.17	215.9835	2600.187	2816.17	-26.00	(21.45)	4.55
4/3/2019	2873.4	14	6	8	70%			1	431.01	2404.522	2835.53	215.505	2595.508	2811.01	-24.52	(21.31)	3.21
4/2/2019	2867.24	13	7	6	65%			1	430.086	2398.763	2828.85	215.043	2590.912	2805.95	-22.89	(21.67)	1.23
4/1/2019	2867.19	14	6	8	70%		1		430.0785	2391.995	2822.07	215.0393	2585.946	2800.99	-21.09	(22.01)	-0.92
3/29/2019	2834.4	13	7	6	65%		1		425.16	2388.952	2814.11	212.58	2583.038	2795.62	-18.49	(22.58)	-4.08
3/28/2019	2815.44	9	11	-2	45%			1	422.316	2388.216	2810.53	211.158	2581.315	2792.47	-18.06	(23.35)	-5.29
3/27/2019	2805.37	3	17	-14	15%			1	420.8055	2388.861	2809.67	210.4028	2580.208	2790.61	-19.06	(24.01)	-4.95
3/26/2019	2818.46	11	9	2	55%		1		422.769	2387.655	2810.42	211.3845	2578.03	2789.41	-21.01	(24.43)	-3.42
3/25/2019	2798.36	6	14	-8	30%		1		419.754	2389.252	2809.01	209.877	2577.182	2787.06	-21.95	(24.59)	-2.64
3/22/2019	2800.71	7	13	-6	35%		1		420.1065	2390.778	2810.88	210.0533	2576.09	2786.14	-24.74	(24.51)	0.23
3/21/2019	2854.88	16	4	12	80%		1		428.232	2384.448	2812.68	214.116	2570.846	2784.96	-27.72	(24.14)	3.58
3/20/2019	2824.23	10	10	0	50%		1		423.6345	2381.599	2805.23	211.8173	2567.475	2779.29	-25.94	(23.51)	2.44
3/19/2019	2832.57	10	10	0	50%		1		424.8855	2376.995	2801.88	212.4428	2563.206	2775.65	-26.23	(23.55)	2.69
3/18/2019	2832.94	17	3	14	85%		1		424.941	2371.524	2796.47	212.4705	2558.563	2771.03	-25.43	(24.06)	1.37
3/15/2019	2822.53	15	5	10	75%		1		423.3795	2366.649	2790.03	211.6898	2554.325	2766.01	-24.01	(25.02)	-1.00
3/14/2019	2808.48	6	14	-8	30%		1		421.272	2363.021	2784.29	210.636	2550.796	2761.43	-22.86	(26.33)	-3.47
3/13/2019	2810.92	11	9	2	55%		1		421.638	2358.387	2780.02	210.819	2546.799	2757.62	-22.41	(27.95)	-5.54
3/12/2019	2791.52	10	10	0	50%		1		418.728	2355.844	2774.57	209.364	2543.932	2753.30	-21.28	(29.65)	-8.37
3/11/2019	2783.3	10	10	0	50%		1		417.495	2354.087	2771.58	208.7475	2541.449	2750.20	-21.39	(31.67)	-10.28
3/8/2019	2743.07	2	18	-16	10%			1	411.4605	2358.053	2769.51	205.7303	2541.782	2747.51	-22.00	(33.78)	-11.78
3/7/2019	2748.93	2	18	-16	10%			1	412.3395	2361.841	2774.18	206.1698	2541.703	2747.87	-26.31	(35.86)	-9.56

S&P Formula Spreadsheet

The last chart for this section provides us with the pivot points and the Fibonacci formula with a few helpful daily and weekly exponential moving averages and pivot points. First let's review the pivot points, pivot points are set up from r2 being the high and s2 being the low, as the issue moves between these points we generate signals up or down as you can see in the location column on the next page. On the chart on the next page you can see on 3/1/18 the pivot point is ps1 that means the issue is in the second lowest bracket to the middle bracket which is p. on 3/9/18 we can see the pivot point level rose from ps1 to pr1 which means the issue rose to the second highest level on the chart as the issue hit the high of the trend. The next box has a few helpful tools to determine resistance levels. On the right side of the box we have the Fibonacci points .236 to 1.618 with the calculation and the resistant point. On the left side of the box we have the pivot points from r2 to s2 and their resistance levels. On the lower have of the box we have the exponential moving averages daily and weekly for the 20 day to the 200 day. Why do we track so many resistance points, we are looking for areas that may have common levels of resistance.

			low	2588.26	0.236	46.80	2635.06
				2786.57	0.382	75.75	2664.01
	move		high	198.31	0.5	99.16	2687.42
					0.618	122.56	2710.82
	r2			2997.43	1	198.31	2786.57
	r1			2855.63	1.618	320.87	2909.13
	p			2694.16			
	s1			2552.36			
	s2			2390.89			
				daily		week	
	exp moving avg			20		20	2683.02
	exp moving avg			50	2711.71	50	2568.93
	exp moving avg			100	2715.85	100	2422.41
	exp moving avg			200	2681.26	200	2215.41
					2598.00		

DATE	CLOSE	total up	total down	c/d	up %	pivots	location	up	down
4/25/2018	2639.4	9	11	-2	45%		ps1		1
4/24/2018	2634.56	7	13	-6	35%		ps1		1
4/23/2018	2670.29	8	12	-4	40%		ps1		1
4/20/2018	2670.14	9	10	-1	47%		r1p		1
4/19/2018	2693.13	9	11	-2	45%		r1p		1
4/18/2018	2708.64	13	7	6	65%		pr1	1	
4/17/2018	2706.39	17	3	14	85%		s1p	1	
4/16/2018	2677.84	16	4	12	80%		ps1	1	
4/13/2018	2656.3	14	6	8	70%		ps1		1
4/12/2018	2663.99	14	6	8	70%		s1p	1	
4/11/2018	2642.19	10	10	0	50%		s1p	1	
4/10/2018	2656.87	13	7	6	65%		s1p		1
4/9/2018	2613.16	6	14	-8	30%		ps1		1
4/6/2018	2604.47	4	16	-12	20%		s1p	1	
4/5/2018	2662.84	13	7	6	65%		s1p	1	
4/4/2018	2644.69	14	6	8	70%		s1p	1	
4/3/2018	2614.45	12	8	4	60%		ps1	1	
4/2/2018	2581.12	2	18	-16	10%		s1p		1
3/29/2018	2640.87	11	9	2	55%		s1p		
3/28/2018	2605	5	15	-10	25%		ps1		1
3/27/2018	2612.62	5	15	-10	25%		ps1		1
3/26/2018	2658.55	8	12	-4	40%		s1p	1	
3/23/2018	2588.26	1	19	-18	5%		ps1		1
3/22/2018	2643.69	3	17	-14	15%		ps1		1
3/21/2018	2711.93	7	13	-6	35%		r1p		1
3/20/2018	2716.94	8	12	-4	40%		r1p		1
3/19/2018	2712.92	7	13	-6	35%		r1p		1
3/16/2018	2752.01	12	8	4	60%		r1p		1
3/15/2018	2747.33	8	12	-4	40%		r1p		1
3/14/2018	2749.48	8	12	-4	40%		r1p		1
3/13/2018	2765.31	11	9	2	55%		r1p		1
3/12/2018	2783.02	13	7	6	65%		pr1	1	
3/9/2018	2786.57	17	3	14	85%		pr1	1	
3/8/2018	2738.97	15	5	10	75%		pr1	1	
3/7/2018	2726.8	8	12	-4	40%		pr1		1

Overall Market Spreadsheet

The over all market spreadsheet is a guide providing us with important information on the overall strength of the market and staying on the right side of the market be it bullish or bearish. We have eight signals for the overall market spreadsheet. First, we have the date and totals for up and down the convergence and divergence column (c/d) is the trigger and the percentage column is the percent between the up and down column 66% is our confirmation that the market is in a uptrend and below 33% for a down trend. Our first formula for the overall market spreadsheet is the Arms index for the NASDAQ, we take the sum of the advancing and declining issues and the advancing and declining volume and divide them to get column M a number over or under 1 is bullish and over 1 is bearish. The highlighted up and down column is the signal for the formula red is down and green is up.

The next formula is the smoothed arms index, that is also called (the open trin) we track the 4, 10, and 21 days for short, medium and long-term moves. The four day is our trigger for all three formulas. We track all three but only use the four day, because of our fast-moving trades, but the 10 and 21 days provide good information that is worth tracking for trending purposes. The four day is calculated the same way as the arms index except, the four day has a four-day moving average of the advancing and declining issue and volume. The smoothing of arms index helps provide less whip saw and more and more of a trend.

Run CTRL-Q from Input Sheet

	Summary				NASDAQ				
	total up	total down	c/d	%	Close	ADV	DEC	ADV Vol	DEC Vol
6/19/2018	1.00	7.00	-6.00	12.50%	7725.59	1265	1696	903930290	1307552840
6/18/2018	2.00	6.00	-4.00	25.00%	7747.03	1526	1425	1145070605	912533800
6/15/2018	0.00	8.00	-8.00	0.00%	7746.38	1483	1452	1354646192	1643554835
6/14/2018	2.00	6.00	-4.00	25.00%	7761.04	1689	1250	1371274450	77577680
6/13/2018	3.00	5.00	-2.00	37.50%	7695.7	1297	1648	1044140522	1103525335
6/12/2018	4.00	4.00	0.00	50.00%	7703.79	1597	1345	1375846744	5898542211
6/11/2018	5.00	3.00	2.00	62.50%	7659.93	1617	1350	1120812304	769105206
6/8/2018	6.00	2.00	4.00	75.00%	7645.51	1528	1396	1161560607	722860192
6/7/2018	4.00	4.00	0.00	50.00%	7635.07	1300	1648	1056431528	1240326251
6/6/2018	5.00	3.00	2.00	62.50%	7689.24	1816	1177	1459382775	687759257
6/5/2018	3.00	5.00	-2.00	37.50%	7637.86	1890	1055	1235157249	731390411
6/4/2018	5.00	3.00	2.00	62.50%	7606.46	1664	1252	1376486884	720590489
6/1/2018	5.00	3.00	2.00	62.50%	7554.33	2080	862	1591674488	569249764
5/31/2018	1.00	7.00	-6.00	12.50%	7442.12	1143	1797	793437765	1695586259
5/30/2018	3.00	5.00	-2.00	37.50%	7462.45	2005	940	1316676099	694406592
5/29/2018	2.00	6.00	-4.00	25.00%	7396.59	1490	1418	936605745	803038696
5/25/2018	1.00	7.00	-6.00	12.50%	7433.85	1490	1418	936605745	803038696
5/24/2018	1.00	7.00	-6.00	12.50%	7424.43	1398	1522	1109151329	893285168
5/23/2018	2.00	6.00	-4.00	25.00%	7425.96	1563	1353	1205853352	751308660
5/22/2018	2.00	6.00	-4.00	25.00%	7378.46	1228	1631	977461417	903224153
5/21/2018	5.00	3.00	2.00	62.50%	7394.04	1737	1132	1188102997	755634784
5/18/2018	1.00	7.00	-6.00	12.50%	7354.34	1390	1409	890675725	980872956
5/17/2018	5.00	3.00	2.00	62.50%	7382.47	1706	1108	876094699	980944409
5/16/2018	4.00	4.00	0.00	50.00%	7398.3	1861	971	1363380734	692201919
5/15/2018	1.00	7.00	-6.00	12.50%	7351.63	1358	1487	872513889	1188817088
5/14/2018	5.00	3.00	2.00	62.50%	7411.32	1308	1564	1218421678	830453384
5/11/2018	4.00	4.00	0.00	50.00%	7402.88	1544	1296	925851204	1121189453
5/10/2018	6.00	2.00	4.00	75.00%	7404.97	1744	1106	1533477145	675044268
5/9/2018	6.00	2.00	4.00	75.00%	7339.91	1770	1109	1457924080	751076705
5/8/2018	4.00	4.00	0.00	50.00%	7266.9	1536	1295	1068479228	952337993
5/7/2018	3.00	5.00	-2.00	37.50%	7265.21	1770	1103	1414043769	493936619
5/4/2018	5.00	3.00	2.00	62.50%	7209.62	2069	765	1608049011	394339790
5/3/2018	2.00	6.00	-4.00	25.00%	7088.15	1014	1816	1015505385	1275316095
5/2/2018	2.00	6.00	-4.00	25.00%	7100.9	1505	1283	977754573	1099404149

	ARMS Index						4 Day ARMS Index			
Issues	Vol		UP	DOWN	ISSUES ADV	ISSUES DEC	VOL Adv	VOL Dec	Issues Adv/Dec	VOL Adv/Dec	ARM Ratio
0.75	0.69	1.08	0	1	5,963	5,823	4,774,921,537	3,941,219,155	1.02	1.21	0.85
1.07	1.25	0.85	1	0	5,995	5,775	4,915,131,769	3,737,191,650	1.04	1.32	0.79
1.02	0.82	1.24	0	1	6,066	5,695	5,145,907,908	8,723,200,061	1.07	0.59	1.81
1.35	17.68	0.08	1	0	6,200	5,593	4,912,074,020	7,848,750,432	1.11	0.63	1.77
0.79	0.95	0.83	1	0	6,039	5,739	4,702,360,177	8,494,032,944	1.05	0.55	1.90
1.19	0.23	5.09	0	1	6,042	5,739	4,714,651,183	8,630,833,860	1.05	0.55	1.93
1.20	1.46	0.82	1	0	6,261	5,571	4,798,187,214	3,420,050,906	1.12	1.40	0.80
1.09	1.61	0.68	1	0	6,534	5,276	4,912,532,159	3,382,336,111	1.24	1.45	0.85
0.79	0.85	0.93	1	0	6,670	5,132	5,127,458,436	3,380,066,408	1.30	1.52	0.86
1.54	2.12	0.73	1	0	7,450	4,346	5,662,701,396	2,708,989,921	1.71	2.09	0.82
1.79	1.69	1.06	0	1	6,777	4,966	4,996,756,386	3,716,816,923	1.36	1.34	1.02
1.33	1.91	0.70	1	0	6,892	4,851	5,078,275,236	3,679,833,104	1.42	1.38	1.03
2.41	2.80	0.86	1	0	6,718	5,017	4,638,394,097	3,762,281,311	1.34	1.23	1.09
0.64	0.47	1.36	0	1	6,128	5,573	3,983,325,354	3,996,070,243	1.10	1.00	1.10
2.13	1.90	1.12	0	1	6,383	5,298	4,299,038,918	3,193,769,152	1.20	1.35	0.90
1.05	1.17	0.90	1	0	5,941	5,711	4,188,216,171	3,250,671,220	1.04	1.29	0.81
1.05	1.17	0.90	1	0	5,679	5,924	4,229,071,843	3,350,856,677	0.96	1.26	0.76
0.92	1.24	0.74	1	0	5,926	5,638	4,480,569,095	3,303,452,765	1.05	1.36	0.77
1.16	1.61	0.72	1	0	5,918	5,525	4,262,093,491	3,391,040,553	1.07	1.26	0.85
0.75	1.08	0.70	1	0	6,061	5,280	3,932,334,838	3,620,676,302	1.15	1.09	1.06
1.53	1.57	0.98	1	0	6,694	4,620	4,318,254,155	3,409,654,068	1.45	1.27	1.14
0.99	0.91	1.09	0	1	6,315	4,975	4,002,665,047	3,842,836,372	1.27	1.04	1.22
1.54	0.89	1.72	0	1	6,233	5,130	4,330,411,000	3,692,416,800	1.22	1.17	1.04
1.92	1.97	0.97	1	0	6,071	5,318	4,380,167,505	3,832,661,844	1.14	1.14	1.00
0.91	0.73	1.24	0	1	5,954	5,453	4,550,263,916	3,815,504,193	1.09	1.19	0.92
0.84	1.47	0.57	1	0	6,366	5,075	5,135,674,107	3,377,763,810	1.25	1.52	0.83
1.19	0.83	1.44	0	1	6,594	4,806	4,985,731,657	3,499,648,419	1.37	1.42	0.96
1.58	2.27	0.69	1	0	6,820	4,613	5,473,924,222	2,872,395,585	1.48	1.91	0.78
1.60	1.94	0.82	1	0	7,145	4,272	5,548,496,088	2,591,691,107	1.67	2.14	0.78
1.19	1.12	1.06	0	1	6,389	4,979	5,106,077,393	3,115,930,497	1.28	1.64	0.78
1.60	2.86	0.56	1	0	6,358	4,967	5,015,352,738	3,262,996,653	1.28	1.54	0.83
2.70	4.08	0.66	1	0	6,264	5,000	4,790,563,526	3,475,553,734	1.25	1.38	0.91
0.56	0.80	0.70	1	0	5,148	6,132	3,707,337,290	4,517,355,898	0.84	0.82	1.02
1.17	0.89	1.32	0	1	5,575	5,687	3,612,939,705	4,345,165,301	0.98	0.83	1.18

Overall market spreadsheet

On the spreadsheet on the next page we have examples of the 10 day and the 21 day Arms Index, along with the 4 day trigger number. The 10 day is a smoothed arms index of 10 days. We calculate this number by taking the arms index over the last 10 days, this provides us with a medium range signal of what the market is doing. The 21 day is a smoothed arms index of 10 days. We calculate this number by taking the arms index over the last 10 days, this provides us with a medium range signal of what the advancing and declining issues along with volume are doing. The 21 day provides us with a long-term signal. On the chart on the next page we can see that all three signals are moving in the same direction down, and a few days later on 6/20/18 the NASDAQ hit the high of the trend 7781.51 and turned down

Tech Smart

	Summary				10 Day ARMS Index										21 Day ARMS Index					ARM Ratio (0.85 or 1.1)	4 Day ARM (.75 or 1.25)	10 Day ARM (.8 or 1.0)
	total up	total down	c/d	%	ISSUES ADV	ISSUES DEC	VOL Adv	VOL Dec	Issues Adv/Dec	VOL Adv/Dec	ARM Ratio	ISSUES ADV	ISSUES DEC	VOL Adv	VOL Dec	Issues Adv/Dec	VOL Adv/Dec					
6/19/2018	1.00	7.00	-6.00	12.50%	15,118	14,387	11,993,096,017	14,363,337,607	1.05	0.83	1.26	32,806	28,767	24,660,309,087	23,684,091,279	1.14	1.04	1.10	0.85	1.26
6/18/2018	2.00	6.00	-4.00	25.00%	15,743	13,746	12,324,322,976	13,787,175,178	1.15	0.89	1.28	32,931	28,480	24,647,054,522	23,357,411,395	1.16	1.06	1.10	0.79	1.28
6/15/2018	0.00	8.00	-8.00	0.00%	15,881	13,573	12,555,739,255	13,595,231,867	1.17	0.92	1.27	33,111	28,163	24,378,078,616	23,425,822,004	1.18	1.04	1.13	1.81	1.27
6/14/2018	2.00	6.00	-4.00	25.00%	16,478	12,983	12,792,767,551	12,520,926,796	1.27	1.02	1.24	33,489	27,682	24,386,813,158	22,474,469,088	1.21	1.09	1.11	1.77	1.24
6/13/2018	3.00	5.00	-2.00	37.50%	15,932	13,530	12,214,930,866	14,138,935,375	1.18	0.86	1.36	33,158	27,919	23,888,052,597	23,585,708,496	1.19	1.01	1.17	1.50	1.36
6/12/2018	4.00	4.00	0.00	50.00%	16,640	12,822	12,487,466,443	13,729,816,632	1.30	0.91	1.43	33,169	27,835	24,062,333,753	23,312,636,545	1.19	1.03	1.35	1.93	1.43
6/11/2018	5.00	3.00	2.00	62.50%	16,533	12,895	12,048,225,444	8,634,313,117	1.28	1.40	0.92	33,116	27,786	23,612,338,213	18,535,283,787	1.19	1.27	0.94	0.80	0.92
6/8/2018	6.00	2.00	4.00	75.00%	16,406	12,963	11,864,018,885	8,668,246,607	1.27	1.37	0.92	33,243	27,542	24,025,003,054	18,441,222,849	1.21	1.30	0.93	0.85	0.92
6/7/2018	4.00	4.00	0.00	50.00%	16,276	13,089	11,811,609,607	8,338,671,583	1.24	1.34	0.93	33,485	27,255	24,321,366,527	18,469,439,362	1.23	1.32	0.93	0.86	0.93
6/6/2018	5.00	3.00	2.00	62.50%	16,539	12,794	11,961,031,431	8,349,653,992	1.29	1.43	0.90	33,721	26,902	24,333,414,227	18,181,451,104	1.25	1.34	0.94	0.82	0.90
6/5/2018	3.00	5.00	-2.00	37.50%	15,951	13,248	11,479,110,073	8,565,118,888	1.20	1.34	0.90	33,675	26,828	24,288,075,221	17,987,628,466	1.26	1.35	0.93	1.02	0.90
6/4/2018	5.00	3.00	2.00	62.50%	15,798	13,325	11,432,055,821	8,589,363,261	1.19	1.33	0.89	33,854	26,538	24,660,966,983	17,650,577,845	1.28	1.40	0.91	1.03	0.89
6/1/2018	5.00	3.00	2.00	62.50%	15,524	13,482	10,946,244,662	8,849,645,728	1.15	1.24	0.93	33,204	27,102	24,299,985,484	18,205,303,451	1.23	1.33	0.92	1.09	0.93
5/31/2018	1.00	7.00	-6.00	12.50%	15,150	13,728	10,230,664,873	9,261,340,373	1.10	1.10	1.00	32,629	27,523	23,686,065,569	18,735,457,836	1.19	1.26	0.94	1.10	1.00
5/30/2018	3.00	5.00	-2.00	37.50%	15,868	12,902	10,800,607,842	8,257,956,033	1.23	1.31	0.94	33,162	26,862	24,081,882,361	17,746,365,277	1.23	1.36	0.90	0.90	0.96
5/29/2018	2.00	6.00	-4.00	25.00%	15,221	13,449	10,356,446,632	8,752,366,529	1.13	1.18	0.96	32,110	27,819	23,290,029,037	18,488,100,639	1.15	1.26	0.92	0.81	0.96
5/25/2018	1.00	7.00	-6.00	12.50%	15,039	13,595	10,638,261,565	8,779,781,217	1.11	1.21	0.91	32,061	27,772	23,274,531,092	18,788,187,441	1.15	1.24	0.93	0.76	0.91
5/24/2018	1.00	7.00	-6.00	12.50%	15,093	13,473	10,627,507,024	9,097,931,974	1.12	1.17	0.96	32,295	27,434	23,808,606,899	18,611,354,305	1.18	1.28	0.92	0.77	0.96
5/23/2018	2.00	6.00	-4.00	25.00%	15,588	13,057	11,051,832,840	8,879,691,074	1.18	1.24	0.95	32,078	27,528	23,582,555,898	18,781,881,560	1.17	1.26	0.93	0.85	0.95
5/22/2018	2.00	6.00	-4.00	25.00%	15,646	12,813	11,303,903,568	8,879,459,119	1.22	1.27	0.96	31,560	27,958	23,187,413,935	19,341,308,614	1.13	1.20	0.94	1.06	0.96
5/21/2018	5.00	3.00	2.00	62.50%	15,954	12,477	11,394,921,379	8,928,572,959	1.28	1.28	1.00	31,508	27,957	22,901,839,696	19,416,912,644	1.13	1.18	0.96	1.14	1.00
5/18/2018	1.00	7.00	-6.00	12.50%	15,987	12,448	11,620,862,151	8,666,874,794	1.28	1.34	0.96	30,839	28,573	22,239,450,063	19,995,978,381	1.08	1.11	0.97	1.22	0.96
5/17/2018	5.00	3.00	2.00	62.50%	16,666	11,804	12,338,235,437	8,080,341,628	1.41	1.53	0.92	30,520	28,995	21,873,439,082	20,438,294,177	1.05	1.07	0.98	1.04	0.92
5/16/2018	4.00	4.00	0.00	50.00%	15,974	12,512	12,477,646,123	8,374,713,314	1.28	1.49	0.86	30,323	29,273	22,082,842,555	20,216,209,510	1.04	1.09	0.95	1.00	0.86
5/15/2018	1.00	7.00	-6.00	12.50%	15,618	12,824	12,092,019,962	8,781,915,544	1.22	1.38	0.88	30,455	29,238	22,161,800,241	19,993,569,433	1.04	1.11	0.94	0.92	0.88
5/14/2018	5.00	3.00	2.00	62.50%	15,936	12,473	12,408,760,630	8,299,592,156	1.28	1.50	0.85	30,976	28,786	22,335,622,050	19,525,313,588	1.08	1.14	0.94	0.83	0.85
5/11/2018	4.00	4.00	0.00	50.00%	15,581	12,806	11,715,161,727	8,905,280,726	1.22	1.32	0.92	30,768	29,013	21,608,470,628	19,943,766,385	1.06	1.08	0.98	0.96	0.92
5/10/2018	6.00	2.00	4.00	75.00%	15,478	12,881	11,710,418,323	8,887,216,771	1.20	1.32	0.91	31,104	28,735	22,105,689,664	19,397,895,448	1.08	1.14	0.95	0.78	0.91
5/9/2018	2.00	6.00	-4.00	25.00%	15,458	12,855	11,647,622,730	8,838,378,063	1.20	1.32	0.91	30,750	29,111	21,352,580,131	19,740,318,031	1.06	1.08	0.98	0.78	0.91
5/8/2018	4.00	4.00	0.00	50.00%	14,869	13,362	11,072,798,978	9,151,113,781	1.11	1.21	0.92	31,333	28,596	21,555,128,330	19,549,574,869	1.10	1.10	0.99	0.78	0.92
5/7/2018	3.00	5.00	-2.00	37.50%	14,378	13,850	10,815,031,139	9,509,511,502	1.04	1.14	0.91	31,316	28,642	21,828,089,788	19,289,345,909	1.09	1.13	0.97	0.83	0.91
5/4/2018	5.00	3.00	2.00	62.50%	13,784	14,377	10,092,874,548	9,994,403,066	0.96	1.01	0.95	30,187	29,828	21,116,111,296	20,428,877,644	1.01	1.03	0.98	0.91	0.95
5/3/2018	2.00	6.00	-4.00	25.00%	12,783	15,360	9,010,538,901	10,934,763,797	0.83	0.82	1.01	29,940	30,141	20,924,817,913	20,727,715,625	0.99	1.01	0.98	1.02	1.01
5/2/2018	2.00	6.00	-4.00	25.00%	12,840	15,375	8,519,698,260	11,082,636,454	0.84	0.77	1.09	31,108	29,066	21,577,980,504	19,995,331,791	1.07	1.08	0.99	1.18	1.09

Overall Market Spreadsheet

The overall market spreadsheet has two arms indexes and open TRIN formulas, one for the NASDAQ, and one for the NYSE. The spreadsheet on the next page provides the 4day arms index (open trin) for the NYSE signal. Next, we use the NYSE advancing and declining numbers for the Dow Jones and the S&P. then, we have the arms index and the up and down signal. We also have the four-day index, which is calculated the same way as the previous spreadsheet, we just use the NYSE, numbers instead of the NASDAQ, numbers.

Run CTRL-Q from Input Sheet

	Summary				4 Day ARM		DOW/S&P		NYSE			
	total up	total down	c/d	%	up	down	DOW	S&P	Adv Issue	DEC Issue	Adv VOL	DEC Vol
6/19/2018	1.00	7.00	-6.00	12.50%	0	1	24700.21	2762.59	1261	1687	1505168187	2085148375
6/18/2018	2.00	6.00	-4.00	25.00%	0	1	24987.47	2773.03	1657	1304	1908408596	1338871222
6/15/2018	0.00	8.00	-8.00	0.00%	0	1	25090.48	2779.66	1403	1546	2223694150	3171844201
6/14/2018	2.00	6.00	-4.00	25.00%	0	1	25175.31	2782.49	1675	1264	1782395524	1681356700
6/13/2018	3.00	5.00	-2.00	37.50%	0	1	25,201.20	2775.63	999	1963	1163719813	2579794776
6/12/2018	4.00	4.00	0.00	50.00%	0	1	25,320.73	2786.85	1463	1482	1801473269	1510543603
6/11/2018	5.00	3.00	2.00	62.50%	0	1	25,322.31	2782	1624	1318	2045512958	1165234811
6/8/2018	6.00	2.00	4.00	75.00%	0	1	25,316.53	2779.03	1740	1219	2056990409	1034033598
6/7/2018	4.00	4.00	0.00	50.00%	0	1	25,241.41	2770.37	1609	1345	2016481095	1672435910
6/6/2018	5.00	3.00	2.00	62.50%	0	1	25,146.39	2772.35	1904	1055	2573273610	1016681034
6/5/2018	3.00	5.00	-2.00	37.50%	0	1	24799.98	2748.8	1769	1200	1893717316	1549053868
6/4/2018	5.00	3.00	2.00	62.50%	0	1	24813.69	2746.87	1929	1022	2057638508	1193164414
6/1/2018	5.00	3.00	2.00	62.50%	0	1	24635.21	2734.62	2092	884	2495050557	1164615006
5/31/2018	1.00	7.00	-6.00	12.50%	0	1	24415.84	2705.27	1094	1885	1111205087	2984766771
5/30/2018	3.00	5.00	-2.00	37.50%	0	1	24667.78	2724.01	2414	574	3035948438	439246915
5/29/2018	2.00	6.00	-4.00	25.00%	0	1	24361.45	2689.86	1354	1585	1035500329	1923581706
5/25/2018	1.00	7.00	-6.00	12.50%	0	1	24753.09	2721.33	1354	1585	1035500329	1923581706
5/24/2018	1.00	7.00	-6.00	12.50%	0	1	24811.76	2727.76	1467	1478	1402425516	1823982712
5/23/2018	2.00	6.00	-4.00	25.00%	0	1	24886.81	2733.29	1528	1402	1472766283	1773863540
5/22/2018	2.00	6.00	-4.00	25.00%	0	1	24834.41	2724.44	1186	1769	1265142862	2067625527
5/21/2018	5.00	3.00	2.00	62.50%	0	1	25013.29	2733.04	2080	896	2162513945	857198000
5/18/2018	1.00	7.00	-6.00	12.50%	0	1	24715.09	2712.97	1506	1424	1243015216	1981973249
5/17/2018	5.00	3.00	2.00	62.50%	0	1	24713.98	2720.13	1592	1345	1927499009	1448484994
5/16/2018	4.00	4.00	0.00	50.00%	0	1	24768.93	2722.46	1923	1030	2210647558	979039050
5/15/2018	1.00	7.00	-6.00	12.50%	0	1	24706.41	2711.45	1072	1890	1288807074	1906635476
5/14/2018	5.00	3.00	2.00	62.50%	0	1	24899.41	2730.13	1411	1551	1554218950	1391118511
5/11/2018	4.00	4.00	0.00	50.00%	0	1	24831.17	2727.72	1628	1310	1496008792	1323141527
5/10/2018	6.00	2.00	4.00	75.00%	0	1	24739.53	2723.07	2126	837	2474612432	791158346
5/9/2018	6.00	2.00	4.00	75.00%	0	1	24542.54	2697.79	1849	1118	2646040621	1124779724
5/8/2018	4.00	4.00	0.00	50.00%	0	1	24360.21	2671.92	1502	1447	1921140963	1700837894
5/7/2018	3.00	5.00	-2.00	37.50%	0	1	24357.32	2672.63	1869	1086	2004928480	1204342302
5/4/2018	5.00	3.00	2.00	62.50%	0	1	24262.51	2663.42	2239	746	2719443396	587435129
5/3/2018	2.00	6.00	-4.00	25.00%	0	1	23930.15	2629.73	1226	1718	1455440898	2357508489
5/2/2018	2.00	6.00	-4.00	25.00%	0	1	23924.98	2635.67	1406	1519	1555676846	2395110037

ARMS Index					4 Day ARMS Index						
Issues	Vol		UP	DOWN	ISSUES ADV	ISSUES DEC	VOL Adv	VOL Dec	Issues Adv/Dec	VOL Adv/Dec	ARM Ratio
0.75	0.72	1.04	0	1	5,996	5,801	7,419,666,457	8,277,220,498	1.03	0.90	1.15
1.27	1.43	0.89	1	0	5,734	6,077	7,078,218,083	8,771,866,899	0.94	0.81	1.17
0.91	0.70	1.29	0	1	5,540	6,255	6,971,282,756	8,943,539,280	0.89	0.78	1.14
1.33	1.06	1.25	0	1	5,761	6,027	6,793,101,564	6,936,929,890	0.96	0.98	0.98
0.51	0.45	1.13	0	1	5,826	5,982	7,067,696,449	6,289,606,788	0.97	1.12	0.87
0.99	1.19	0.83	1	0	6,436	5,364	7,920,457,731	5,382,247,922	1.20	1.47	0.82
1.23	1.76	0.70	1	0	6,877	4,937	8,692,258,072	4,888,385,353	1.39	1.78	0.78
1.43	1.99	0.72	1	0	7,022	4,819	8,540,462,430	5,272,204,410	1.46	1.62	0.90
1.20	1.21	0.99	1	0	7,211	4,622	8,541,110,529	5,431,335,226	1.56	1.57	0.99
1.80	2.53	0.71	1	0	7,694	4,161	9,019,679,991	4,923,514,322	1.85	1.83	1.01
1.47	1.22	1.21	0	1	6,884	4,991	7,557,611,468	6,891,600,059	1.38	1.10	1.26
1.89	1.72	1.09	0	1	7,529	4,365	8,699,842,590	5,781,793,106	1.72	1.50	1.15
2.37	2.14	1.10	0	1	6,954	4,928	7,677,704,411	6,512,210,398	1.41	1.18	1.20
0.58	0.37	1.56	0	1	6,216	5,629	6,218,154,183	7,271,177,098	1.10	0.86	1.29
4.21	6.91	0.61	1	0	6,589	5,222	6,509,374,612	6,110,393,039	1.26	1.07	1.18
0.85	0.54	1.59	0	1	5,703	6,050	4,946,192,457	7,445,009,664	0.94	0.66	1.42
0.85	0.54	1.59	0	1	5,535	6,234	5,175,834,990	7,589,053,485	0.89	0.68	1.30
0.99	0.77	1.29	0	1	6,261	5,545	6,302,848,606	6,522,669,779	1.13	0.97	1.17
1.09	0.83	1.31	0	1	6,300	5,491	6,143,438,306	6,680,660,316	1.15	0.92	1.25
0.67	0.61	1.10	0	1	6,364	5,434	6,598,171,032	6,355,281,770	1.17	1.04	1.13
2.32	2.52	0.92	1	0	7,101	4,695	7,543,675,728	5,266,695,293	1.51	1.43	1.06
1.06	0.63	1.69	0	1	6,093	5,689	6,669,968,857	6,316,132,769	1.07	1.06	1.01
1.18	1.33	0.89	1	0	5,998	5,816	6,981,172,591	5,725,278,031	1.03	1.22	0.85
1.87	2.26	0.83	1	0	6,034	5,781	6,549,682,374	5,599,934,564	1.04	1.17	0.89
0.57	0.68	0.84	1	0	6,237	5,588	6,813,647,248	5,412,053,860	1.12	1.26	0.89
0.91	1.12	0.81	1	0	7,014	4,816	8,170,880,795	4,630,198,108	1.46	1.76	0.83
1.24	1.13	1.10	0	1	7,105	4,712	8,537,802,808	4,939,917,491	1.51	1.73	0.87
2.54	3.13	0.81	1	0	7,346	4,488	9,046,722,496	4,821,118,266	1.64	1.88	0.87
1.65	2.35	0.70	1	0	7,459	4,397	9,291,553,460	4,617,395,049	1.70	2.01	0.84
1.04	1.13	0.92	1	0	6,836	4,997	8,100,953,737	5,850,123,814	1.37	1.38	0.99
1.72	1.66	1.03	0	1	6,740	5,069	7,735,489,620	6,544,395,957	1.33	1.18	1.12
3.00	4.63	0.65	1	0	6,433	5,369	7,284,213,946	5,536,430,421	1.20	1.32	0.91
0.71	0.62	1.16	0	1	5,299	6,472	5,688,695,529	7,515,500,672	0.82	0.76	1.08
0.93	0.65	1.43	0	1	5,773	6,011	5,951,735,826	6,590,880,972	0.96	0.90	1.06

Overall Market Spreadsheet

The spreadsheet on the next page provides the summary of the overall market, the up, down, c/d, and percentage of the market. We also have the 10 day and 21 day arms index (open TRIN), along with the totals of the 4 day, 10 day, and the 21 day and the up and down signal. looking at the ratio column of the 4, 10, 21 day right before the up and down column (BT, BU, BV,) we can see our trigger numbers on the top of each column. The three smoothed formulas all have different signals, and this is true for both the NASDAQ and the NYSE. The trigger for the 4 day is if the ratio is below .75 this is bullish and if the ratio is above 1.25 this is a bearish signal. the 10 day trigger is when the ratio is below .80 this is bullish and when the ratio is above 1.0 the market is bearish. The 21 day trigger is when the ratio falls below .85 the market is bullish and when the ratio is above 1.1 the market is bearish as you can see in the spreadsheet.

Run CTRL-Q from Input Sheet

	Summary				10 Day ARMS Index						
	total up	total down	c/d	%	ISSUES ADV	ISSUES DEC	VOL Adv	VOL Dec	Issues Adv/Dec	VOL Adv/Dec	ARM Ratio
6/19/2018	1.00	7.00	-6.00	12.50%	15,335	14,183	19,077,117,611	17,255,944,230	1.08	1.11	0.98
6/18/2018	2.00	6.00	-4.00	25.00%	15,843	13,696	19,465,666,740	16,719,849,723	1.16	1.16	0.99
6/15/2018	0.00	8.00	-8.00	0.00%	16,115	13,414	19,614,896,652	16,574,142,915	1.20	1.18	1.02
6/14/2018	2.00	6.00	-4.00	25.00%	16,804	12,752	19,886,253,059	14,566,913,720	1.32	1.37	0.97
6/13/2018	3.00	5.00	-2.00	37.50%	16,223	13,373	19,215,062,622	15,870,323,791	1.21	1.21	1.00
6/12/2018	4.00	4.00	0.00	50.00%	17,638	11,984	21,087,291,247	13,729,775,930	1.47	1.54	0.96
6/11/2018	5.00	3.00	2.00	62.50%	17,529	12,087	20,321,318,307	14,142,814,033	1.45	1.44	1.01
6/8/2018	6.00	2.00	4.00	75.00%	17,259	12,354	19,311,305,678	14,901,160,928	1.40	1.30	1.08
6/7/2018	4.00	4.00	0.00	50.00%	16,986	12,613	18,656,740,785	15,691,110,042	1.35	1.19	1.13
6/6/2018	5.00	3.00	2.00	62.50%	16,905	12,670	18,113,025,973	15,792,537,672	1.33	1.15	1.16
6/5/2018	3.00	5.00	-2.00	37.50%	16,187	13,384	16,804,895,225	16,843,482,165	1.21	1.00	1.21
6/4/2018	5.00	3.00	2.00	62.50%	16,498	13,080	17,073,691,854	16,151,626,297	1.26	1.06	1.19
6/1/2018	5.00	3.00	2.00	62.50%	16,075	13,482	16,259,068,562	16,940,435,132	1.19	0.96	1.24
5/31/2018	1.00	7.00	-6.00	12.50%	15,575	13,943	15,691,517,014	17,224,305,120	1.12	0.91	1.23
5/30/2018	3.00	5.00	-2.00	37.50%	16,404	13,088	16,790,959,485	15,218,577,399	1.25	1.10	1.14
5/29/2018	2.00	6.00	-4.00	25.00%	15,062	14,404	15,043,818,121	16,685,965,960	1.05	0.90	1.16
5/25/2018	1.00	7.00	-6.00	12.50%	15,119	14,370	15,562,536,742	16,153,502,765	1.05	0.96	1.09
5/24/2018	1.00	7.00	-6.00	12.50%	15,393	14,095	16,023,045,205	15,553,062,586	1.09	1.03	1.06
5/23/2018	2.00	6.00	-4.00	25.00%	16,052	13,454	17,095,232,121	14,520,238,220	1.19	1.18	1.01
5/22/2018	2.00	6.00	-4.00	25.00%	16,373	13,170	18,268,506,459	13,871,154,404	1.24	1.32	0.94
5/21/2018	5.00	3.00	2.00	62.50%	16,689	12,848	18,924,504,560	13,504,366,771	1.30	1.40	0.93
5/18/2018	1.00	7.00	-6.00	12.50%	16,478	13,038	18,766,919,095	13,851,511,073	1.26	1.35	0.93
5/17/2018	5.00	3.00	2.00	62.50%	17,211	12,360	20,243,347,275	12,456,972,953	1.39	1.63	0.86
5/16/2018	4.00	4.00	0.00	50.00%	16,845	12,733	19,771,289,164	13,365,996,448	1.32	1.48	0.89
5/15/2018	1.00	7.00	-6.00	12.50%	16,328	13,222	19,116,318,452	14,782,067,435	1.23	1.29	0.95
5/14/2018	5.00	3.00	2.00	62.50%	16,818	12,718	19,381,164,184	13,071,808,725	1.32	1.48	0.89
5/11/2018	4.00	4.00	0.00	50.00%	16,512	13,016	18,950,870,213	14,247,195,594	1.27	1.33	0.95
5/10/2018	6.00	2.00	4.00	75.00%	16,584	12,963	19,173,342,616	14,356,942,856	1.28	1.34	0.96
5/9/2018	6.00	2.00	4.00	75.00%	16,458	13,107	19,018,387,274	14,876,224,316	1.26	1.28	0.98
5/8/2018	4.00	4.00	0.00	50.00%	15,897	13,662	18,139,456,775	15,505,322,964	1.16	1.17	0.99
5/7/2018	3.00	5.00	-2.00	37.50%	15,445	14,113	17,616,429,623	16,071,381,696	1.09	1.10	1.00
5/4/2018	5.00	3.00	2.00	62.50%	14,907	14,615	17,173,671,701	16,283,403,179	1.02	1.05	0.97
5/3/2018	2.00	6.00	-4.00	25.00%	13,647	15,830	15,604,886,021	17,912,609,991	0.86	0.87	0.99
5/2/2018	2.00	6.00	-4.00	25.00%	13,328	16,125	15,415,456,259	17,654,296,481	0.83	0.87	0.95

						21 Day ARMS Index				
ISSUES ADV	ISSUES DEC	VOL Adv	VOL Dec	Issues Adv/Dec	VOL Adv/Dec	21 ARM Ratio (0.85 or 1.1)	4 day .75 /1.25	10day .80 / 1.0	up	down
33,602	28,463	38,044,526,781	34,956,624,395	1.18	1.09	1.08	1.15	0.98	0	1
33,847	28,200	37,782,373,810	34,853,449,269	1.20	1.08	1.11	1.17	0.99	0	1
33,782	28,241	37,801,464,223	34,963,063,041	1.20	1.08	1.11	1.14	1.02	0	1
34,302	27,725	37,788,417,631	32,770,257,890	1.24	1.15	1.07	0.98	0.97	0	1
33,699	28,351	37,294,829,181	32,995,536,666	1.19	1.13	1.05	0.87	1.00	0	1
34,111	27,939	37,685,328,318	31,806,860,401	1.22	1.18	1.03	0.82	0.96	0	1
34,276	27,767	37,379,863,841	31,619,458,325	1.23	1.18	1.04	0.78	1.01	0	1
34,778	27,286	37,808,963,315	31,245,381,860	1.27	1.21	1.05	0.90	1.08	0	1
34,887	27,185	38,398,013,527	31,336,127,986	1.28	1.23	1.05	0.99	1.13	0	1
34,780	27,287	38,302,673,395	31,364,529,970	1.27	1.22	1.04	1.01	1.16	0	1
34,745	27,318	37,734,328,265	31,552,191,238	1.27	1.20	1.06	1.26	1.21	0	1
35,215	26,864	38,560,054,345	30,590,572,499	1.31	1.26	1.04	1.15	1.19	0	1
34,512	27,560	37,957,856,735	31,754,916,574	1.25	1.20	1.05	1.20	1.24	0	1
33,826	28,195	37,018,483,024	32,985,411,605	1.20	1.12	1.07	1.29	1.23	0	1
34,294	27,696	37,460,930,743	30,197,021,600	1.24	1.24	1.00	1.18	1.14	0	1
32,985	28,971	35,548,907,284	32,324,280,065	1.14	1.10	1.04	1.42	1.16	0	1
33,331	28,643	36,231,888,150	31,833,587,148	1.16	1.14	1.02	1.30	1.09	0	1
33,977	28,039	37,516,044,911	31,220,445,248	1.21	1.20	1.01	1.17	1.06	0	1
33,798	28,234	37,880,729,517	31,150,340,908	1.20	1.22	0.98	1.25	1.01	0	1
33,320	28,730	37,806,077,045	31,643,373,994	1.16	1.19	0.97	1.13	0.94	0	1
33,465	28,549	38,103,104,741	30,992,112,252	1.17	1.23	0.95	1.06	0.93	0	1
32,364	29,614	37,091,248,512	32,351,556,193	1.09	1.15	0.95	1.01	0.93	0	1
31,765	30,203	37,114,244,432	32,468,777,923	1.05	1.14	0.92	0.85	0.86	0	1
31,799	30,167	37,249,931,979	32,325,813,711	1.05	1.15	0.91	0.89	0.89	0	1
32,037	29,930	37,415,671,747	32,123,770,487	1.07	1.16	0.92	0.89	0.95	0	1
33,116	28,854	38,306,721,746	31,032,202,084	1.15	1.23	0.93	0.83	0.89	0	1
32,979	28,956	37,966,631,070	31,348,474,198	1.14	1.21	0.94	0.87	0.95	0	1
32,957	28,997	38,260,943,429	31,250,930,804	1.14	1.22	0.93	0.87	0.96	0	1
32,318	29,603	37,274,188,878	31,965,178,849	1.09	1.17	0.94	0.84	0.98	0	1
32,713	29,220	37,718,974,786	31,306,389,476	1.12	1.20	0.93	0.99	0.99	0	1
32,620	29,288	37,262,996,105	31,114,062,392	1.11	1.20	0.93	1.12	1.00	0	1
31,378	30,516	35,566,638,869	32,855,375,818	1.03	1.08	0.95	0.91	0.97	0	1
31,287	30,560	35,403,000,557	32,898,011,970	1.02	1.08	0.95	1.08	0.99	0	1
32,093	29,759	36,388,983,319	31,411,646,055	1.08	1.16	0.93	1.06	0.95	0	1

Overall Market Spreadsheet

Our final section of the overall market spreadsheet provides us with some information I like to follow closely let's start with the VIX. We track the close of the VIX and the percentage of the move from the previous day and of the currant day. Generally, as the VIX raises the market falls and vice a versa. The stock making new highs and the stocks making new lows is one of my favorite formulas and maybe because it is my own formula. We install the high /low of the NYSE and the NASDAQ and incorporate that data into one formula. we use the daily ratio and then smooth it by 10 days to provide less whip saw and more of a short-term trend. The last signal is the NYSE and the NASDAQ working in conjunction to form a signal. The trigger is the 10 day of the NYSE and the NASDAQ smoothed over 10 day again for less whip saw. The last three columns are the total up and total down of the three signals of the high low formula and the total up or down. Last is the DOW, S&P, NASDAQ closing numbers.

A	B	C	D	E	BY	BZ	CA	CB	CC	CD	CE	CF	CG	CH	CI	CJ
Run CTRL-Q from Input Sheet																
		Summary											NYSE			
	total up	total down	c/d	%	VIX	Chg	Chg % Prev	Chg % Current	up	down	high	low	Ratio	10 day average	up	down
6/19/2018	1.00	7.00	-6.00	12.50%	12.73	-1.58	-11%	-12%	1	0	59	82	0.72	3.38	0	1
6/18/2018	2.00	6.00	-4.00	25.00%	14.31	1.23	9%	9%	0	1	105	79	1.33	3.65	0	1
6/15/2018	0.00	8.00	-8.00	0.00%	13.08	0.46	4%	4%	0	1	85	68	1.25	4.05	0	1
6/14/2018	2.00	6.00	-4.00	25.00%	12.62	-0.16	-1%	-1%	1	0	101	53	1.91	4.21	0	1
6/13/2018	3.00	5.00	-2.00	37.50%	12.78	0.69	6%	5%	0	1	210	31	6.77	4.17	1	0
6/12/2018	4.00	4.00	0.00	50.00%	12.09	-0.51	-4%	-4%	1	0	130	29	4.48	3.88	1	0
6/11/2018	5.00	3.00	2.00	62.50%	12.60	0.1	1%	1%	0	1	146	25	5.84	3.48	1	0
6/8/2018	6.00	2.00	4.00	75.00%	12.50	-0.63	-5%	-5%	1	0	115	22	5.23	2.95	1	0
6/7/2018	4.00	4.00	0.00	50.00%	13.13	1.67	15%	13%	0	1	166	57	2.91	2.56	1	0
6/6/2018	5.00	3.00	2.00	62.50%	11.46	-0.61	-5%	-5%	1	0	175	52	3.37	2.34	1	0
6/5/2018	3.00	5.00	-2.00	37.50%	12.07	-0.59	-5%	-5%	1	0	175	52	3.37	2.33	1	0
6/4/2018	5.00	3.00	2.00	62.50%	12.66	-0.8	-6%	-6%	1	0	166	31	5.35	2.33	1	0
6/1/2018	5.00	3.00	2.00	62.50%	13.46	-1.19	-8%	-9%	1	0	112	39	2.87	1.95	1	0
5/31/2018	1.00	7.00	-6.00	12.50%	14.65	-0.13	-1%	-1%	1	0	101	66	1.53	2.51	0	1
5/30/2018	3.00	5.00	-2.00	37.50%	14.78	1.56	12%	11%	0	1	155	40	3.88	2.58	1	0
5/29/2018	2.00	6.00	-4.00	25.00%	13.22	0	0%	0%	1	0	3	6	0.50	2.27	0	1
5/25/2018	1.00	7.00	-6.00	12.50%	13.22	0.21	2%	2%	0	1	3	6	0.50	2.61	0	1
5/24/2018	1.00	7.00	-6.00	12.50%	13.01	0.09	1%	1%	0	1	66	48	1.38	3.01	0	1
5/23/2018	2.00	6.00	-4.00	25.00%	12.92	-1.36	-10%	-11%	1	0	35	55	0.64	3.31	0	1
5/22/2018	2.00	6.00	-4.00	25.00%	14.28	1.29	10%	9%	0	1	134	41	3.27	3.51	0	1
5/21/2018	5.00	3.00	2.00	62.50%	12.99	-0.43	-3%	-3%	1	0	191	57	3.35	3.30	1	0
5/18/2018	1.00	7.00	-6.00	12.50%	13.42	0.17	1%	1%	0	1	112	72	1.56	3.16	0	1
5/17/2018	5.00	3.00	2.00	62.50%	13.25	-0.3	-2%	-2%	1	0	450	53	8.49	3.12	1	0
5/16/2018	4.00	4.00	0.00	50.00%	13.55	-0.93	-6%	-7%	1	0	124	54	2.30	2.32	0	1
5/15/2018	1.00	7.00	-6.00	12.50%	14.48	1.4	11%	10%	0	1	68	100	0.68	2.20	0	1
5/14/2018	5.00	3.00	2.00	62.50%	13.08	0.43	3%	3%	0	1	123	31	3.97	2.17	1	0
5/11/2018	4.00	4.00	0.00	50.00%	12.65	-0.53	-4%	-4%	1	0	113	25	4.52	1.92	1	0
5/10/2018	6.00	2.00	4.00	75.00%	13.18	-0.41	-3%	-3%	1	0	140	32	4.38	1.60	1	0
5/9/2018	6.00	2.00	4.00	75.00%	13.59	-0.91	-6%	-7%	1	0	152	59	2.58	1.24	1	0
5/8/2018	4.00	4.00	0.00	50.00%	14.50	-0.47	-3%	-3%	1	0	80	67	1.19	1.00	1	0
5/7/2018	3.00	5.00	-2.00	37.50%	14.97	0.2	1%	1%	0	1	113	59	1.92	0.94	1	0
5/4/2018	5.00	3.00	2.00	62.50%	14.77	-1.1	-7%	-7%	1	0	75	64	1.17	0.81	1	0
5/3/2018	2.00	6.00	-4.00	25.00%	15.87	-0.34	-2%	-2%	1	0	56	121	0.46	0.74	0	1
5/2/2018	2.00	6.00	-4.00	25.00%	16.21	0.82	5%	5%	0	1	75	65	1.15	0.77	1	0

CK	CL	CM	CN	CO	CP	CQ	CR	CS	CT	CU	CV	CV	CX	CY	CZ	DA
		NASDAQ					NEW HIGHS									
						NYSE Ratio/NASDAQ Ratio	NYSE 10 DayRatio/NASDAQ 10 Day Ratio	combo same way								
high	low	Ratio	10 day average	up	down				up	down						
143	51	2.80	5.85	0	1	0.26	0.58		0	1	0	3	-3	24,700.21	2762.59	7,725.59
191	47	4.06	6.25	0	1	0.33	0.58		0	1	0	3	-3	24,987.47	2773.03	7,747.03
165	43	3.84	6.54	0	1	0.33	0.62		0	1	0	3	-3	25,090.48	2779.66	7,746.38
194	35	5.54	6.67	0	1	0.34	0.63		0	1	0	3	-3	25,175.31	2782.49	7,761.04
104	33	3.15	6.44	0	1	2.15	0.65		1	0	2	1	1	25,201.20	2775.63	7,695.70
207	31	6.68	6.68	0	1	0.67	0.58		1	0	2	1	1	25,320.73	2786.85	7,703.79
199	27	7.37	6.31	1	0	0.79	0.55		1	0	3	0	3	25,322.31	2782	7,659.93
148	16	9.25	5.87	1	0	0.57	0.50		1	0	3	0	3	25,316.53	2779.03	7,645.51
276	31	8.90	5.20	1	0	0.33	0.49		0	1	2	1	1	25,241.41	2770.37	7,635.07
268	39	6.87	4.50	1	0	0.49	0.52		0	1	2	1	1	25,146.39	2772.35	7,689.24
268	39	6.87	4.21	1	0	0.49	0.55		0	1	2	1	1	24,799.98	2748.8	7,637.86
248	36	6.89	4.04	1	0	0.78	0.58		1	0	3	0	3	24,813.69	2746.87	7,606.46
197	38	5.18	3.70	1	0	0.55	0.53		1	0	3	0	3	24,635.21	2734.62	7,554.33
159	49	3.24	3.52	0	1	0.47	0.71		0	1	0	3	-3	24,415.84	2705.27	7,442.12
211	38	5.55	3.42	1	0	0.70	0.76		0	1	2	1	1	24,667.78	2724.01	7,462.45
113	38	2.97	3.00	0	1	0.17	0.75		0	1	0	3	-3	24,361.45	2689.86	7,396.59
113	38	2.97	3.16	0	1	0.17	0.83		0	1	0	3	-3	24,753.09	2721.33	7,433.85
117	47	2.49	3.20	0	1	0.55	0.94		0	1	0	3	-3	24,811.76	2727.76	7,424.43
90	47	1.91	3.37	0	1	0.33	0.98		0	1	0	3	-3	24,886.81	2733.29	7,425.96
167	42	3.98	3.44	1	0	0.82	1.02		0	1	1	2	-1	24,834.41	2724.44	7,378.46
202	39	5.18	3.25	1	0	0.65	1.02		0	1	2	1	1	25,013.29	2733.04	7,394.04
148	42	3.52	3.22	1	0	0.44	0.98		0	1	1	2	-1	24,715.09	2712.97	7,354.34
170	50	3.40	3.06	1	0	2.50	1.02		1	0	3	0	3	24,713.98	2720.13	7,382.47
146	67	2.18	2.79	0	1	1.05	0.83		1	0	1	2	-1	24,768.93	2722.46	7,398.30
93	65	1.43	2.73	0	1	0.48	0.81		0	1	0	3	-3	24,706.41	2711.45	7,351.63
141	31	4.55	2.63	1	0	0.87	0.82		1	0	3	0	3	24,899.41	2730.13	7,411.32
150	45	3.33	2.31	1	0	1.36	0.83		1	0	3	0	3	24,831.17	2727.72	7,402.88
177	42	4.21	2.08	1	0	1.04	0.77		1	0	3	0	3	24,739.53	2723.07	7,404.97
177	69	2.57	1.76	1	0	1.00	0.70		1	0	3	0	3	24,542.54	2697.79	7,339.91
119	57	2.09	1.55	1	0	0.57	0.64		0	1	2	1	1	24,360.21	2671.92	7,266.90
128	26	4.92	1.40	1	0	0.39	0.67		0	1	2	1	1	24,357.32	2672.63	7,265.21
90	48	1.88	0.98	1	0	0.63	0.83		0	1	2	1	1	24,262.51	2663.42	7,209.62
62	84	0.74	0.88	0	1	0.63	0.84		0	1	0	3	-3	23,930.15	2629.73	7,088.15
83	51	1.63	0.95	1	0	0.71	0.81		0	1	2	1	1	23,924.98	2635.67	7,100.90

WORLD MARKETS

The major US Markets and the world markets are interconnected. If anyone fails or has success it will impact the other connected markets, so we feel it is important to track the trend of the main world markets and see how it correlates with our markets. We track the yearly data on our summary spreadsheet to avoid whip saw, but it is important to keep an eye on the daily trend as you can see on the next page. Looking at the spreadsheet on the next page we have the date and the daily and yearly summary the yearly summary is our signal. The world markets we track are the overall global market which consist of ; the global dow (world),the global dow euro (world), dj global index (world), dj global ex u.s (world). The global data has 4 signals daily and yearly.

Countries have several signals but for now we will just name the countries, and the number of signals per country Australia (2) china (3) India (1) Indonesia(1) japan (3) Malaysia (1) New Zealand (1) Philippines(1) Singapore(1) south Korea (1) Sri Lanka (1) Taiwan (1) Thailand (1).

The next is Europe we have 24 daily and yearly signals; Europe (4) Austria, Belgium, Czech Republic, Denmark, Finland, France, Germany, Hungery, Italy, Netherlands, Norway, Poland, Portugal, Russia, Spain, Sweden, Switzerland, Turkey, U.K. (2)

Next, we have the Americas we have six signals ; DJ Americas, Argentina, Brazil, Canada, Chile, and Mexico. The last section is called other countries and there are two signals; Israel and south Africa. There could be up to 54 signals depending on which markets are open that day. The variance section in the summary area is the signal, in the yearly column we highlighted the change in variance (chg. in var) that is the trigger for the summary spreadsheet

How to Pick Top Stocks

With all the stocks out there, it can be very confusing as to, just where to start, so we are going to make it simple. We are going to pick the all-star team of stock, why not have the strongest stocks working for us. But one key to remember is don't fall in love with a stock. When a stock turns get rid of it. We can buy it again when it regains the criteria we are looking for. How do we find these all stars? We have six ways of finding strong stocks that are trending up. Here is how we do it ; 1, top sectors 2, sector leaders 3, top 50 stocks 4, global leaders, 5, big cap 20, 6, stocks in the spot light. now that we know where to find the stock lets break down how we do it.

Top sectors

We want to select stocks in the top 5 to 10 sectors. These sectors will usually outperform the S&P. On the spreadsheet on the next page the first column is the sectors rated from one to ten every week we update the sector data from the Investor Business Daily. On the spread sheet on page 106 you can see on 6/25/18 business service was ranked sixth and on 6/29/18 the business service sector moved up to second this is a sector on the move. We track the top ten, but we look at all the sectors to see if any are trending up.

Sector Leaders

Sector leaders are the all-stars of the stock market and if we can stay in the top five sectors these stocks should out preform the S&P. The Investor Business Daily (IBD) has a sector leader page or you can look through the sector sections and pick the sector leaders. They will be highlighted in the sector and boxed out. Now just because it is a sector leader we don't just buy it we have to check the trend of the stock and the accumulation of the stock at the time you are investing. We only invest in stocks that have A or B rating. This means the stock is being accumulated this is very important do not buy a stock that has less a b rating.

Top 50 stock

Top 50 stocks are a computer generated watch list of market leading growth stocks. We focus on the top 10 stocks while watching the stock that are on the move upwards from 50 to 1. The first thing and most important thing is that the stock has a B or better accumulated / distribution ratting. The top 50 are generated by evaluating earnings, sales, price action and other basics.

Global leaders

The global leader is listed in the (IBD) from one to ten, and they are some of the strongest companies on the globe. We use the global leaders as a guide to see if and sector leaders are global leaders. On the spreadsheet on page 106 you can see Boazun is a sector leader and a global leader.

Big cap 20

The big cap 20 is large cap stocks that are ranked from one to twenty. We look at big cap stocks and watch the stocks that are trending up the ladder to number one. We also use the big cap twenty as a guide to help pick strong stocks. The big cap twenty is a computer generated watch list of large cap stocks by Investor's Business Daily (IBD)

Stocks in the Spot Light

The stocks in the spot light are generated by the (IBD), they look for stocks that have strong, earnings, sale and other fundamentals. These stocks are also in a base or breakout status that usually provide a uptrend. When checking the spreadsheet on the next page we can see several sector leaders in the stocks in the spot light. We do not look at any stocks that have less than a b rating for accumulation / distribution.

Conclusion

Now we know where to find the stocks. We want sector leaders in the top five sectors. We want top 50 and big cap 20 stocks that are on the move, (meaning trending bullish). Then we check global leaders and stocks in the spot light to see if any of our potential stock pick are in more than one category. The most important thing is to buy stocks that have A, B or greater accumulation / distribution ratting. Stocks that are being accumulated are more likely to rise over stocks that are not being accumulated.

		6/25/2018															
		sector		top 50			sector leader		top 5					global leaders			
147		software	1	abiomed	abmd	heart assist	b	1	palo alto	panw	network security	b		1	melanox tech	mlnx	semiconductor
148		apparel	2	trade desk inc cla	ttd	data platform	b+	1	salesforce	crm	software	b		2	alibaba	baba	cloud
149		medical	3	twitter	twtr	real time content	b+	1	servicenow	now	software	b		3	momo inc	momo	social network
150		consumer	4	align technology	algn	treating teeth	b	1	adobe sys	adbe	software	b		4	auto home	atm	website auto
151		retail	5	canada goose	goos	retailer	a-	2	ultimather	ulti	payroll software	a-		5	orion engineered carbns	oec	makes carbon
152		business svc	6	netflix	nflx	internet tv	a-	2	canada goose	goos	retailer	a-		6	globant	globant	carbon coatings
153		leisure	7	five below	five	retail stores	a-	3	abiomed	abmd	heart assist	a-		7	zto express	zto	express delivery service
154		internet	8	huazhu group ads	htht	chinese lodging	a-	3	align technology	algn	treating teeth	a-		8	htht	htht	chinese lodging
155		alcohl/tob	9	grubhub	grub	restaurants	a-	3	alibaba	baba	cloud	a-		9	atlassian	team	software cloud
156		computer	10	kemet corp	kem	electronics	a-		arista networks	anet	software	a-		10	boxun	bzun	marketing
157									facebook	fb	stay connected	a-					
158								5	five below	five	retail stores	a-					
159								6	health equity	heq	tech/tax	a					
160								7	netflix	nflx	internet tv	b					
161									yy inc	yy	stay connected	b					
162																	
163																	
164		6/29/2018															
165		sector		top 50			sector leader		top 5					global leaders			
166		software	1	abiomed	abmd	heart assist	b	1	bozun	bzun	marketing	c		1	melanox tech	mlnx	semiconductor
167		business svc	2	trade desk inc cla	ttd	data platform	b	1	palo alto	panw	network security	c+		2	ferrari	race	formula 1
168		medical	3	grubhub	grub	restaurants	c+	1	salesforce	crm	software	b-		3	momo inc	momo	social network
169		consumer	4	twitter	twtr	real time content	b+	1	servicenow	now	software	c-		4	auto home	atm	website auto
170		apparel	5	align technology	algn	treating teeth	b	1	adobe sys	adbe	software	b		5	orion engineered carbns	oec	makes carbon
171		retail	6	canada goose	goos	retailer	b	2	health equity	heq	pharmaceuticals	c		6	globant	globant	carbon coatings
172		alcohl/tob	7	netflix	nflx	internet tv	b-	3	supreplm	supn	heart assist	b+		7	zto express	zto	express delivery service
173		energy	8	five below	five	retail stores	a-	3	abiomed	abmd	treating teeth	b-		8	huazhu group ads	htht	chinese lodging
174		leisure	9	supreplm	supn	pharmaceuticals	a-	3	align technology	algn	retailer	b-		9	atlassian	team	software cloud
175		internet	10	kemet corp	kem	electronics	b	5	canada goose	goos	retail stores	a-		10	bozun	bzun	marketing
176								6	five below	five	stay connected	a-					
177									facebook	fb	social networking	b					
178									momo inc	momo	national bank fz	b-					
179									seacoast banking	sbcf							

Tech Smart 165

sector leader	spot light	stock	symble	type	price	price	percent	rating strength in sector	ranking	stock pass	checkup neutral	fail	ranking
1		salesforce	crm	software	136.4	141.4	4%	71		28	1	1	
1		five below	five	etail store	97.71	98.9	1%	5		26	2	2	
1		health quilty	hqy	tech/tax	75.1	78.55	5%	12		27	2	1	
1		abiomed	abmd	heart assis	409.05	405.99	-1%	67		28	1	1	
1	1	supnsphrm	supn	armaceuti	59.85	52.4	-12%	134		28		2	
		twitter	twtr	l time con	43.67	46.65	7%	40		24	1	5	
1	1	align technology	algn	eating tee	342.14	347.47	2%	69		26	1	3	
1	1	netflix	nflx	internet tv	391.43	408.25	4%	8		25	2	3	
1		canada goose	goos	retailer	58.85	59.61	1%	17		26	1	3	
1	1	ligand pharmaceuticals	lgnd	armaceuti	207.17	216.67	5%	144		26	1	3	
							15%						1.5%

sector leader	spot light	stock	symble	type	price	price	percent	rating strength in sector	ranking	stock pass	checkup neutral	fail	ranking
		salesforce	crm	software	141.4	147.31	4%	65		26	2	2	
	1	five below	five	etail store	98.9	101.36	2%	5		25	2	3	
		health quilty	hqy	tech/tax	78.55	80.23	2%	10		27	2	1	
	1	regenxbio	rgnx	virus gene	79.3	77.35	-2%	94		26		4	
	1	upland software	upld	lops cloud	36.68	35.66	-3%	43		24	1	5	
		twitter	twtr	l time con	46.65	44.49	-5%	43		22	1	7	
		align technology	algn	eating tee	347.47	363.45	5%	75		28	1	1	
		netflix	nflx	internet tv	408.25	395.8	-3%	9		25	2	3	
		canada goose	goos	retailer	59.61	60.27	1%	14		26	1	3	
	1	ligand pharmaceuticals	lgnd	armaceuti	216.67	221.09	2%	10		27	1	3	
							4%						0.36%

How to Analyze A Stock

We now have our top stocks from our top sectors. Let's put them to the test and make sure they are as strong as we think. A great tool to use is the IBD stock checkup. On the chart on the next page we can see the first group of categories, we want to check. Next to each rating we have a number, that number is the percentile ranking within the group.

Composite Rating

The IBD smart select composite rating combines all 5 smarts select ratings into one easy to use rating. A 99 rating means the stock out performed 99% of all the stocks in its group in terms of its combined smart select ratings

EPS Rating

EPS rating is ranked from 1 to 99 scale it ranks all companies publicly traded, comparing earnings per share and growth.

Relative Strength Rating

The relative strength rating or relative price strength is a corporate rating that measures the stock price performance over the last twelve months compared to all other stocks in the IBD'S database

SMR Rating

The SMR rating is a proprietary rating pioneered by the investors business daily. This rating helps identify companies with superior sales, growth, profit margins and return on equity ratios.

Accumulation / Distribution Rating

The accumulation / distribution rating is one of the IBD'S smart select corporate ratings, it tracks the relative degree of institutional buying and selling in a stock over the last 13 weeks

Industry Group Rating

The industry group rating is a proprietary number of the Investor's Business Daily the short version, is obtained by calculations on pricing and weighted time periods over all stocks in the industry. the rating is ranked from 1 to 197.

Estimate Revision

An IBD proprietary formula that looks at estimate earnings growth for the current quarter, year, and next year.

Tech Smart

stock	symble	type	price	price	percent
salesforce	crm	software	138.41	135.01	-2%
boazun	bzun	marketing	62.83	60.82	-3%
health quilty	hqy	tech/tax	81.01	80.63	0%
abiomed	abmd	heart assist	443.58	427.29	-4%
servicenow	now	software	186.35	176.7	-5%
twitter	twtr	real time content	45.8	45.88	0%
align technology	algn	treating teeth	362.66	353.27	-3%
netflix	nflx	internet tv	391.98	411.09	5%
ultrimts software	ulti	software	279.98	267.87	-4%
adobe sys	adbe	software	251.82	243.63	-3%
					-2.0%

						stock checkup	stock checkup	stock checkup	
	rating strength in sector	ranking				pass	neutral	fail	ranking
	78					28		2	5
	5	1				27	1	2	
	10	4				28	1	1	3
	69					29		1	2
	72					29	1		1
	51	5				25		5	
	72					27		3	
	6	2				26	1	3	
	16					26		4	
	7	3				28		2	4

stock	symble	type	price	price	percent
salesforce	crm	software	136.4	141.4	4%
five below	five	retail stores	97.71	98.9	1%
health quilty	hqy	tech/tax	75.1	78.55	5%
abiomed	abmd	heart assist	409.05	405.99	-1%
supnsphrm	supn	pharmaceuticals	59.85	52.4	-12%
twitter	twtr	real time content	43.67	46.65	7%
align technology	algn	treating teeth	342.14	347.47	2%
netflix	nflx	internet tv	391.43	408.25	4%
canada goose	goos	retailer	58.85	59.61	1%
ligand pharmaceuticals	lgnd	pharmaceuticals	207.17	216.67	5%
					1.5%

				stock pass	neutral	fail	
71				28	1	1	
5				26	2	2	
12				27	2	1	
67				28	1	1	
134				28		2	
40				24	1	5	
69				26	1	3	
8				25	2	3	
17				26	1	3	
144				26	1	3	

15%

The next few sections on the spreadsheet on the next page are; the stock checkup score and where we find the stocks themselves along with the stock name the symbol, type of stock price from the previous week and the new price for the current week and last the percentage gain for that week. When we look at the spreadsheet we can see some of the stocks are listed in multiple categories, this is a good signal. When gathering our information if there is a choice between two stocks and everything is equal pick the stock that is in multiple categories.

Stock Checkup

The first column is the stock checkup, we use the composite rating in the specific sector for this ranking. We feel the composite rating is the best indicator to juMdge the overall strength of the stock.

Top Sector

The top sector is generally the most important area where we try to find our stock pick. The IBD ranks the sectors from 1 to 33. In this scenario we want to try to pick a stock from the top 5 categories as long as all the other signals are good. The stock checkup ranks the stocks industry group from 1 to 197. We want to try to pick stock in the top 50 categories. We can pick stocks outside of this guideline so long as all the other indicators are working and moving in the right direction.

World Leaders

The IBD lists the world leaders every week from 1 to 10. It also provides weekly and year to date percentages. When looking at World Leader stocks, to make sure the country the stock is from is trending in the same direction as your investment. We always want to be on the same side as the market.

Top 50

The top 50 is a computer generated list of market leading growth stocks. When reviewing the stock on the top 50 list we want to watch stocks that are on the move up the ladder, and that are being accumulated, with A, B or better. The IBD also provides a chart of all the top 50 stocks with a 10 week moving average indicator. Along with volume and a moving average volume indicator. The IBD also provides buy points, breakouts, profit taking points cup and handle and other technical analysis.

Big cap 20

The big cap 20 is a computer generated list of leading growth stocks that the IBD generates on a weekly basis. The IBD uses strong price action, earnings, sales and other fundamentals to generate this watch list.

sector leader	spot light	stock	symble	type	price	price	percent		rating strength in sector	ranking	stock pass	checkup neutral	fail	ranking
1		salesforce	crm	software	136.4	141.4	4%		71		28	1	1	
1		five below	five	retail store	97.71	98.9	1%		5		26	2	2	
1		health quilty	hqy	tech/tax	75.1	78.55	5%		12		27	2	1	
1		abiomed	abmd	heart assis	409.05	405.99	-1%		67		28	1	1	
1	1	supnsphrm	supn	armaceuti	59.85	52.4	-12%		134		28		2	
		twitter	twtr	l time cont	43.67	46.65	7%		40		24	1	5	
	1	align technology	algn	eating tee	342.14	347.47	2%		69		26	1	3	
1	1	netflix	nflx	internet tv	391.43	408.25	4%		8		25	2	3	
1	1	canada goose	goos	retailer	58.85	59.61	1%		17		26	1	3	
	1	ligand pharmaceuticals	lgnd	armaceuti	207.17	216.67	5%		144		26	1	3	
							15%	1.5%						

sector leader	spot light	stock	symble	type	price	price	percent		rating strength in sector	ranking	stock pass	checkup neutral	fail	ranking
		salesforce	crm	software	141.4	147.31	4%		65		26	2	2	
	1	five below	five	retail store	98.9	101.36	2%		5		25	2	3	
		health quilty	hqy	tech/tax	78.55	80.23	2%		10		27	2	1	
	1	regenxbio	rgnx	virus gene	79.3	77.35	-2%		94		26		4	
	1	upland software	upld	ops cloud	36.68	35.66	-3%		43		24	1	5	
		twitter	twtr	l time cont	46.65	44.49	-5%		43		22	1	7	
		align technology	algn	eating tee	347.47	363.45	5%		75		28	1	1	
		netflix	nflx	internet tv	408.25	395.8	-3%		9		25	2	3	
		canada goose	goos	retailer	59.61	60.27	1%		14		26	1	3	
	1	ligand pharmaceuticals	lgnd	armaceuti	216.67	221.09	2%		10		27	1	3	
							4%	0.36%						

Sector Leaders

The sector leaders are the All Star team of the stock world. These stocks out preform all other stocks in their categories. This is the first place we start when looking for stocks to buy. But remember, all stock trend from bullish to bearish. Make sure all the other indicators and signals are supporting and confirming your pick

Spot Light Stocks

The Stock Spot Light looks at stock that are in a base or breaking out. The stocks they pick have strong earnings, sales and other fundamentals. The IBD also provides a chart with a 10 week moving average along with volume and a moving average of the volume. The IBD also provides technical analysis such as buy points, breakouts, profit taking points cup and handle to name a few.

Stock

The stock column is just the stock name that we have picked. The next two columns are the symbol and type of stock. The symbol is the stocks three or four letters that identify a stock in the market. The type of stock is the sector the stock is in.

Price / Percent

The price column is the price from last week and the price from the current week. We monitor the stocks on a daily and weekly basis and make our changes weekly. The percent column is the percent of the weekly change. Any stock that is under performing we cut and change out with new up and coming stocks from the categories we listed previously in this book. On the bottom of the page we have a percent of the ten stocks we picked. Next to the total percent we have a average percent between the 10 stocks so we can track how we are doing against the S&P 500 or any other stock or index

Stock check up

The stock checkup is a great tool, it gives us so much useful information to analyze our stocks. We put together a rating strength in sector calculation. We did this by adding the composite rating, EPS rating, RS rating, ACC/DIS rating of a stock in its sector and then we rank the stock from 1 to 10 to see if there is a trend. The second half of the stock check up that we look at is the pass, neutral, and fail information. The stock checkup has 30 signals that provides useful information on the strength of a stock we are looking at. The stock checkup has a total of 30 signals, so the high score is 30, we count the pass, neutral, and failed signals we are looking for a stock, with a 25 or greater score. We will get more in depth with the stock check up in the next few pages.

Tech Smart

stock	symbol	type	price	price	percent		rating strength in sector	ranking	stock pass	checkup neutral	fail	ranking
salesforce	crm	software	138.41	135.01	-2%		75		28		2	3
boazun	bzun	marketing	62.83	60.82	-3%		5	1	27	1	2	
health quilty	hqy	tech/tax	81.01	80.63	0%		10	3	28	1	1	5
abiomed	abmd	heart assist	443.58	427.29	-4%		69		29		1	1
servicenow	now	software	186.35	176.7	-5%		72		29	1		2
twitter	twtr	real time content	45.8	45.88	0%		51	5	25		5	
align technology	algn	treating teeth	362.66	353.27	-3%		72		26	1	3	
netflix	nflx	internet tv	391.98	411.09	5%		8	2	26		4	
ultrimts software	ulti	software	279.98	267.87	-4%		16	4	28		2	4
					-17%	-2%						
salesforce	crm	software	136.4	141.4	4%		71		28	1	1	1
five below	five	retail stores	97.71	98.9	1%		5	1	26	2	2	
health quilty	hqy	tech/tax	75.1	78.55	5%		12	3	27	2	1	4
abiomed	abmd	heart assist	409.1	405.99	-1%		67		28	1	1	2
supnsphrm	supn	pharmaceuticals	59.85	52.4	-12%		134		28		2	3
twitter	twtr	real time content	43.67	46.65	7%		40	5	24	1	5	
align technology	algn	treating teeth	342.1	347.47	2%		69		26	1	3	5
netflix	nflx	internet tv	391.4	408.25	4%		8	2	25	2	3	
canada goose	goos	retailer	58.85	59.61	1%		17	4	26	1	3	
ligand pharmaceuticals	lgnd	pharmaceuticals	207.2	216.67	5%		144		26	1	3	
					15%	1.5%						

Stock check up

The IBD stock checkup is a great tool to use when checking on a stock. The first thing is to put the stock symbol in the get stock checkup tab on the top of the page. The stock information will be generated along with the top five stocks in the sector for the specific ratings EPS, RSR ACC/DIS etcetera. The ratings are listed across the top of the page starting with composite rating, EPS rating, relative strength rating, SMR rating, and finishing with the ACC / DIS rating.

When pressing a tab in any one of the rating tabs provide your stocks rating in the sector and the top four in that sector if your stock is not in the top five. The IBD also provides a chart of your stock to the right by hitting the chart symbol. The chart provides volume, 50 day moving average, average daily volume, market cap, 52 week high. The chart also provides daily or weekly and inter day charting, and at the bottom of the page it provides some news from The IBD for your stock pick. Under the top five rating the IBD give a brief description of the stocks function. The stock checkup has six main categories and the composite rating. We focus on the composite rating and the ACC/DIS rating as a key factor in our stock rating sectors but let's review all the sections because they are all important.

Market direction and industry group for your stock

General market; provides the direction of the general market itself.

Industry group ranking (1 to 197); provides the ranking of your stock

Group RS RATING; Provides the fundamental quality of a stocks industry

Fundamental Performance for your stock & Current Earnings

EPS due date: estimated date of next earning report

EPS rating: the IBD rates a stock from 1 to 99 if a stock has a 90 rating this means the stock our performed 90% of the stock in its group

EPS% change (last quarter): compares last quarter's earnings growth with a year ago quarter's earnings growth

Last 3 quarters average EPS growth: calculated average growth for the last 3 quarters

Number of quarters of EPS acceleration: the number of quarters where quarterly earnings growth sequential acceleration in the rate of growth

EPS estimate% change (current quarter): the current quarters estimated earnings growth compared to the quarter a year ago

Estimated revision: an IBD proprietary formula that looks at estimated earnings growth for the current quarter current year and next year

Last quarter % earnings surprise; when a quarterly or annual report is above or below estimated earnings

Annual Earnings

3years EPS growth rate; the compound 3 year growth rate calculated using the last squares fit over the last two to three years earnings per share on a running 12 month basis. Growth rate will be calculated only if there is a minimum of eight trailing 4 quarters periods of positive earnings (uses a minimum of 11 quarters of data)

Consecutive years of annual EPS growth: the number of years that the annual growth increases from the prior year

EPS estimate % change for current year: estimate annual growth for the current year

Sales, Margin, ROE

SMR rating; a proprietary rating pioneered by the IBD to identify companies with superior sales growth profit margins and return on equity ratio

Sales % change (last quarter): compares change from the same quarter last year, blue is equal or greater and red is a decrease in sales

3 years sales growth rate: calculated using the least squares fit over the last three years of sales history on a trailing 4 quarter basis.

Annual pre tax margin: calculated by dividing annual income by annual sales

Annual ROE: equals net income / shareholder's equity

Debt / equity ratio: is the proportion of equity and debt the company is using to finance its assets

Technical Performance for a stock

Price and Volume

Price; is the price of the stock at the end of the business day

Rs rating; the IBD smart select corporate rating is a measure of a stock's price performance over the last twelve months compared to all stocks in the database

% off of 52 week high; it provides the percentage away from the 52 week high current stock price is located

Price vs. 50 day moving average; the price above or below the 52 week moving average in percentage format

50 day average volume; the average number of shares traded over the last 50 days

Supply and Demand

Market capitalization; the total market value of a company

Accumulation / distribution rating : an exclusive rating in the IBD that tracks the buying (accumulating) and selling (distribution) of institutions over the last 13 weeks. The ranking is from A to E A meaning heavy buying and E is heavy selling

Up / down volume ratio: over 50 days divide the up volume by the down volume. A signal over 1 implies positive demand for the stock

% change in # funds owning stock: in the last quarter, the percentage change in the number of funds owning the stock

Quarters of increasing fund ownership: the number of consecutive quarters where mutual funds ownership has increased

Chart for the Stock

On the bottom of the page the IBD provides a stock chart at a glance. This chart provides a daily and weekly view with a 10 week moving average along with a relative strength line as per the close of the day. On the bottom of the chart it has the volume of the day or week depending on the chart you desire with a moving average of the volume over a set period

IBD Articles for the Stock

On the right of the chart the IBD provides articles of the stock we are researching over the last week or two. There is a tab on the bottom of the page (view all) that will provide news and analysis of the stock and the sector we are researching.

Perfect Storm Tracking Results

Mar 28, 2018 through April 12, 2019

		Current YTD 4/12/2019		2018 Actual 3/29/18 to 12/31/18		Since Inception 3/29/2018	
S&P Return		16.0%	2,907.41	-6.7%	2,506.85	10.1%	2,640.87
Selections		24.4%		27.2%		58.2%	
	Performance Above S&P	8.4%		33.9%		48.1%	
Portfolio Value		$ 158,179		$ 127,155		$ 100,000	
Cash Available	83,594.84						

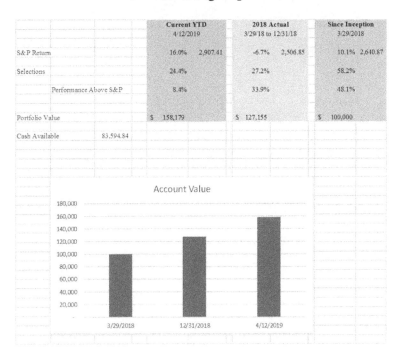

Account Value

DETAILS OF SELECTIONS

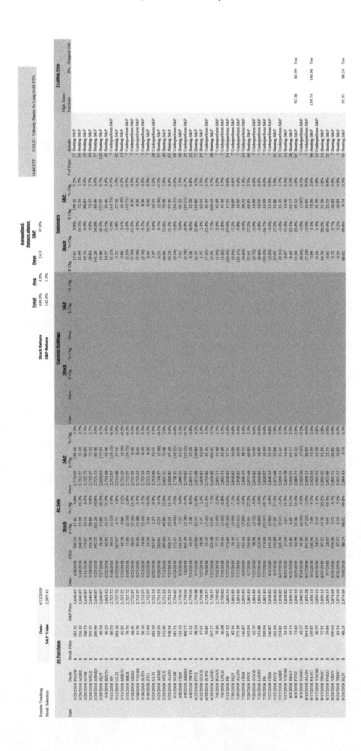

Tech Smart

Results Tracking																Stock Return		Total	Avg	Annualized Return above S&P							
Stock Selection	Date:	4/1/2019																4.69%	4.8%	47.8%							
	S&P Value	2,907.41														S&P Return		142.0%	1.5%								
																									Gold ETF	UGLD - VelocityShares 3x Long Gold ETN	
	At Purchase					At Sale				Stock	Current Holdings		S&P		Summary					High Since	Trailing Stop						
Date	Stock	Stock Price	S&P Price	Date	Price	S&P Price	Stock $ Chg	Stock % Chg	Price	S&P $ Chg	S&P % Chg	Stock $ Chg	Stock % Chg	S&P $ Chg	S&P % Chg	Days	# of Days	Results		Purchase	8% Stopped Out						
9/7/2018	AMD	27.38	2,871.68	9/14/2018	32.72	2,904.98	5.34	19.6%				32.70	1.1%				7	Beating S&P		100.33	Yes						
9/7/2018	INFN	10.85	2,871.68	9/14/2018	28792	2,904.98	19.07	7.3%				32.70	1.1%				7	Beating S&P		254.87	Yes						
9/7/2018	SPLK	44.74	2,871.68	9/14/2018	49.33	2,904.98	4.59	10.3%				32.70	1.1%				7	Beating S&P		214.30	Yes						
9/7/2018	WWE	87.02	2,871.68	9/14/2018	88.40	2,904.98	1.38	1.6%				32.70	1.1%				7	Beating S&P		352.54	Yes						
9/14/2018	ADBE	266.92	2,904.38	10/8/2018	260.33	2,884.43	(6.59)	-2.5%				(19.95)	-0.7%				24	Underperform S&P		39.79	Yes						
9/14/2018	VEEV	74.69	2,904.38	10/8/2018	54.87	2,884.43	(19.82)	-7.2%				(19.95)	-0.7%				24	Underperform S&P		100.33	Yes						
9/21/2018	PANW	239.52	2,929.67	10/5/2018	214.30	2,885.57	(15.22)	-6.6%				(44.10)	-1.5%				14	Underperform S&P		277.03	Yes						
9/21/2018	NFLX	363.19	2,929.67	10/5/2018	352.54	2,885.57	(8.65)	-2.8%				(44.10)	-1.5%				14	Underperform S&P		232.93	Yes						
9/21/2018	RNG	41.72	2,929.67	10/8/2018	39.79	2,885.57	(1.93)	-4.6%				(44.10)	-1.5%				17	Underperform S&P		383.2	Yes						
9/21/2018	MOMO	46.44	2,929.67	10/29/2018	43.80	2,613.08	(2.64)	-5.7%				(143.99)	-4.9%				38	Underperform S&P		43.25	Yes						
9/28/2018	AMD	449.75	2,913.98	10/23/2018	422.97	2,925.51	(26.78)	-6.0%				11.53	0.4%				25	Beating S&P		422.97	Yes						
9/28/2018	ALGN	391.22	2,913.98	10/4/2018	366.97	2,901.61	(24.25)	-6.2%				(12.37)	-0.4%				6	Underperform S&P		366.97	Yes						
10/05/2018	ADBE	248.87	2,767.13	10/24/2018	240.79	2,656.10	(8.08)	-3.2%				(111.03)	-4.0%				15	Beating S&P		261.73	Yes						
10/12/2018	BOX	83.48	2,767.13	10/24/2018	81.83	2,656.10	(1.64)	-2.0%				(111.03)	-4.0%				12	Beating S&P		88.94	Yes						
10/12/2018	ALGN	211.95	2,767.13	10/19/2018	195.31	2,767.78	(16.64)	-7.9%				0.65	0.0%				7	Underperform S&P		212.29	Yes						
10/12/2018	MOMO	37.65	2,767.13	10/19/2018	35.42	2,809.21	(2.23)	-5.9%				42.08	1.5%				7	Beating S&P		38.5	Yes						
1/4/2019	SERV	85.69	2,549.69	1/18/2019	90.50	2,670.71	4.81	5.6%				121.02	4.7%				14	Underperform S&P		100	Yes						
1/4/2019	CRM	137.96	2,549.69	4/12/2019	160.71	2,907.10	22.75	16.5%				357.72	14.0%				98	Beating S&P		150.48	Yes						
1/4/2019	NOW	179.23	2,549.69	1/31/2019	210.14	2,704.10	30.91	17.2%				154.41	6.1%				27	Beating S&P		210.14	Yes						
1/11/2019	INVA	19.39	2,596.26	1/30/2019	18.30	2,681.05	(1.09)	-5.6%				84.79	3.3%				19	Underperform S&P		20.54	Yes						
2/1/2019	CRM	155.87	2,706.53	4/12/2019	160.71	2,907.10	4.84	3.1%				200.69	7.4%				70	Underperform S&P		163.57	Yes						
1/4/2019	TEAM	98.98	2,549.69	4/5/2019	111.33	2,892.14	12.35	12.5%				190.42	7.0%				69	Beating S&P		117.06	Yes						
2/1/2019	NOW	223.51	2,702.32	2/15/2019	234.09	2,775.60	13.38	6.0%				73.28	2.7%				14	Beating S&P		237.49	Yes						
2/1/2019	PANW	220.27	2,702.32	5/10/2019	230.08	2,881.40	9.81	4.5%				179.08	6.6%				29	Beating S&P		230.08	Yes						
2/1/2019	CRM	145.26	2,702.32	2/8/2019	148.18	2,707.88	2.11	2.1%				5.56	0.2%				7	Beating S&P		74.45	Yes						
2/1/2019	TTD	78.50	2,702.32	2/15/2019	83.11	2,775.60	4.21	5.5%				73.28	2.7%				14	Beating S&P		86.83	Yes						
2/8/2019	FTNT	58.20	2,707.88	3/1/2019	61.30	2,803.69	3.19	3.5%				95.81	3.5%				21	Beating S&P		95.99	Yes						
2/8/2019	NOW	215.71	2,707.88	2/15/2019	220.85	2,775.60	5.15	2.4%				67.72	2.5%				7	Beating S&P		122.73	Yes						
2/15/2019	ADBE	362.06	2,775.60	3/1/2019	348.06	2,803.69	(14.00)	-3.9%				28.09	1.0%				14	Underperform S&P		352.6	Yes						
2/15/2019	ANET	33.59	2,775.60	3/27/2019	35.27	2,731.02	1.68	5.0%				(32.53)	-1.2%				39	Beating S&P		274.97	Yes						
2/15/2019	SSNC	59.76	2,775.60	3/8/2019	57.44	2,743.07	(2.32)	-3.9%				(44.54)	-1.3%				35	Underperform S&P		62.43	Yes						
2/22/2019	SSNC	53.60	2,792.67	3/8/2019	58.86	2,743.07	(4.64)	14.3%				(44.54)	-1.3%				14	Underperform S&P		59.88	Yes						
2/22/2019	ANET	214.97	2,792.67	3/29/2019	314.66	2,834.40	39.49	14.4%				41.73	1.5%				35	Beating S&P			-						
2/22/2019	EQY	80.39	2,792.67	3/1/2019	83.28	2,803.69	2.89	3.6%				11.02	0.4%				7	Beating S&P		64.36	Yes						
2/22/2019	SSNC	59.88	2,792.67	3/8/2019	57.44	2,743.07	(2.44)	-4.1%				(49.60)	-1.8%				14	Underperform S&P		59.21	Yes						
3/1/2019	NOW	243.52	2,803.69	3/8/2019	240.49	2,743.07	(3.03)	-1.2%				(49.60)	-1.8%				7	Beating S&P									
3/1/2019	ADBE	262.14	2,803.69	5/1/2019	62.30	2,923.73	0.16	0.3%				120.02	4.3%				60	Underperform S&P		67.72	Yes						
3/22/2019	PAGS	29.59	2,800.71	4/4/2019	29.11	2,879.39	(0.48)	-1.6%				78.68	2.8%				13	Underperform S&P		31.64	Yes						
3/22/2019	AMZN	1,764.77	2,800.71	3/29/2019	1,780.75	2,834.40	15.98	0.9%				33.69	1.2%				7	Underperform S&P									
4/5/2019	ANET	311.66	2,892.74	4/30/2019	306.93	2,845.83	(4.11)	-1.3%				53.09	1.8%				25	Underperform S&P		331.27	Yes						
4/5/2019	KLAC	124.34	2,892.74	4/12/2019	123.45	2,907.41	(0.91)	-0.7%				14.67	0.5%				7	Underperform S&P		124.34	Yes						

Portfolio Performance

			SKP			100,000.00	Acct Value	110,692.89					
								4/12/2019		S&P Ending Balance		2,906.81	2,907.41
								3/29/2018		% Return for S&P		-6.70%	16.0%
								2,640.87	S&P	2,907.41	10.1%	% Return for Trading Selections	27.10%	24.4%
			Trading	(1,199,560.00)	1,282,634.84	83,948.84	100,000.00	31,594.84	4,583.73	126,178.57	58.2%	Performance Above S&P	33.80%	8.4%
											43.31%	43.33%	43.1%	Trading Account Ending Balance	1,527,155.00	158,318.57

At Purchase				Cash Out	Cash In	Cash Available	Invested	Realized Gain/Loss	Unrealized Gain/Loss	Acct Value	Gain/Loss Above S&P
Date	Stock	Stock Price	S&P Price								
3/29/2018 PANW	$ 181.52	2,640.87	(10,000.00)	10,000.00	100,000.00						
3/29/2018 ADBE	$ 216.10	2,640.87	(10,000.00)	10,681.18		981.18		9.8%			
3/29/2018 NOW	$ 168.73	2,640.87	(10,000.00)	11,017.58		1,017.58		10.2%			
3/29/2018 NFLX	$ 295.35	2,640.87	(10,000.00)	10,600.96		600.96		6.0%			
3/29/2018 ABMD	$ 290.99	2,640.87	(10,000.00)	10,978.12		978.12		9.8%			
3/29/2018 HQY	$ 69.14	2,640.87	(10,000.00)	13,479.84		3,479.84		34.8%			
3/4/2018 BZUN	$ 48.23	2,664.42	(10,000.00)	12,619.78		2,619.78		26.2%			
5/1/2018 BZ	$ 60.51	2,727.72	(10,000.00)	13,150.27		3,150.27		31.5%			
5/11/2018 LLTI	$ 243.16	2,727.72	(10,000.00)	9,910.54		(89.46)		-1.0%			
5/11/2018 MELI	$ 41.92	2,727.72	(10,000.00)	10,173.98		173.98		1.7%			
5/11/2018 EBIX	$ 79.70	2,727.72	(10,000.00)	10,205.15		205.15		2.1%			
5/18/2018 SEDG	$ 66.43	2,712.97	(10,000.00)	9,736.51		(263.49)		-2.6%			
5/18/2018 SLPH	$ 31.78	2,712.97	(10,000.00)	8,871.33		(1,128.67)		-11.3%			
5/18/2018 VNDA	$ 36.10	2,712.97	(10,000.00)	9,585.76		(434.24)		-4.3%			
5/18/2018 ZTD	$ 17.60	2,712.97	(10,000.00)	9,625.67		(374.33)		-3.7%			
5/25/2018 LLTI	$ 265.50	2,721.33	(10,000.00)	11,954.55		1,954.55		19.5%			
5/25/2018 ADBE	$ 243.56	2,721.33	(10,000.00)	10,069.27		69.27		0.7%			
5/25/2018 NFLX	$ 351.60	2,721.33	(10,000.00)	10,019.28		19.28		0.2%			
6/1/2018 ALGN	$ 353.54	2,721.33	(10,000.00)	11,276.35		1,276.35		12.8%			
6/1/2018 NOW	$ 173.33	2,734.62	(10,000.00)	11,110.98		1,110.98		11.1%			
6/8/2018 GRMN	$ 450.77	2,779.03	(10,000.00)	10,561.42		561.42		5.6%			
6/8/2018 TWTR	$ 41.21	2,779.03	(10,000.00)	9,907.73		(92.27)		-0.9%			
6/22/2018 FIVE	$ 98.54	2,754.88	(10,000.00)	10,769.82		769.82		7.7%			
6/22/2018 GOOG	$ 57.61	2,718.37	(10,000.00)	13,382.84		3,382.84		33.8%			
6/29/2018 SLPN	$ 59.15	2,718.37	(10,000.00)	10,237.81		237.81		2.4%			
6/29/2018 LGND	$ 207.17	2,718.37	(10,000.00)	10,767.97		767.97		7.7%			
7/6/2018 RNDX	$ 39.50	2,759.82	(10,000.00)	8,755.22		(1,244.78)		-12.4%			
7/6/2018 UPLD	$ 36.68	2,759.82	(10,000.00)	10,787.97		(245.92)		-2.5%			
7/13/2018 FB	$ 207.32	2,801.31	(15,000.00)	9,724.10		2,402.50		15.0%			
7/20/2018 HQY	$ 82.34	2,801.83	(15,000.00)	11,177.48		(321.23)		-4.6%			
7/20/2018 ALGN	$ 371.18	2,801.83	(10,000.00)	9,590.00		(410.00)		-4.1%			
7/20/2018 GRM	$ 146.87	2,801.83	(10,000.00)	12,858.30		2,858.30		28.3%			
7/20/2018 FIVE	$ 102.84	2,801.83	(10,000.00)	7,600.07		(631.08)		-6.3%			
7/20/2018 GOOG	$ 62.79	2,801.83	(10,000.00)	5,248.84		1,315.07		13.2%			
7/20/2018 FB	$ 251.58	2,801.83	(6,580.00)	5,398.24		(211.50)		-3.8%			
7/20/2018 LGND	$ 209.94	2,801.83	(10,000.00)	4,648.41		(984.80)		-16.7%			
7/27/2018 CRM	$ 146.87	2,818.82	(5,000.00)	9,563.65		(396.95)		-4.0%			
7/27/2018 FIVE	$ 102.84	2,818.82	(10,000.00)	12,711.17		2,711.17		27.1%			
7/27/2018 ADBE	$ 254.51	2,818.82	(10,000.00)	9,642.41		(357.52)		-3.6%			
7/27/2018 VNDA	$ 23.42	2,818.82	(10,000.00)	11,098.14		1,098.14		11.0%			
8/3/2018 HEAT	$ 51.15	1,840.35	(10,000.00)	11,208.80		1,208.80		12.1%			
8/3/2018 ETSY	$ 53.63	1,840.35	(10,000.00)	11,342.83		1,342.83		15.4%			
8/10/2018 NNBR	$ 42.27	1,856.13	(10,000.00)	9,895.91		(104.09)		-1.0%			
8/17/2018 ALGN	$ 343.53	1,856.13	(10,000.00)	10,598.34		(98.34)		1.4%			
8/17/2018 PAYC	$ 139.87	1,856.13	(10,000.00)	10,590.90		590.90		5.9%			
8/17/2018 TREE	$ 72.91	1,856.13	(10,000.00)	10,140.73		140.73		1.4%			
8/17/2018 VEEV	$ 19.84	1,856.13	(10,000.00)	10,024.41		2,024.41		10.2%			
8/24/2018 PXGO	$ 89.40	1,856.13	(10,000.00)	14,541.31		4,541.31		45.4%			
8/24/2018 TREE	$ 100.64	2,874.69	(10,000.00)	10,249.82		349.63		3.7%			
8/24/2018 HQY	$ 82.34	1,874.69	(10,000.00)	10,518.56		519.96		5.2%			
			(10,000.00)	19,975.07		9,975.07		99.8%			

			S&P		100,000.00	Acct Value			110,092.89	Gains/Loss		S&P Ending Balance	End 2018	2019 YTD
					3/29/2018				4/12/2019	Above S&P			2,506.83	2,907.41
					2,640.87	S&P			2,907.41			% Return for S&P	-6.79%	16.0%
			Trading	(1,199,060.00)	1,282,654.84	83,594.84	53,594.84	4,583.73	158,178.57	48,085.69	48.1%	% Return for Trading Selections	27.10%	24.4%
												Performance Above S&P	33.89%	8.4%
				Cash Out	Cash In	Cash Available	Invested	Realized Gain/Loss	Unrealized Gain/Loss	Acct Value		Trading Account End'rs Balance	$ 127,155.00	158,178.57
At Purchase														
Date	Stock	Stock Price	S&P Price		100,000.00									
9/7/2018	AMD	27.38	2,871.68	(10,000.00)	11,986.33			1,986.33			19.9%			
9/7/2018	INGN	269.85	2,871.68	(10,000.00)	10,722.78			722.78			7.2%			
9/7/2018	SFIX	44.74	2,871.68	(10,000.00)	11,025.93			1,025.93			10.3%			
9/7/2018	WWE	87.02	2,871.68	(10,000.00)	10,158.58			158.58			1.6%			
9/14/2018	VEEV	106.92	2,904.38	(10,000.00)	9,333.65			(616.35)			-6.2%			
9/14/2018	ADBE	273.69	2,904.38	(10,000.00)	9,273.48			(726.52)			-7.3%			
9/21/2018	PANW	229.32	2,929.67	(10,000.00)	9,339.88			(660.12)			-6.6%			
9/21/2018	NFLX	361.19	2,929.67	(10,000.00)	9,760.51			(239.49)			-2.4%			
9/21/2018	VNDM	41.72	2,929.67	(10,000.00)	9,537.39			(462.61)			-4.6%			
9/28/2018	ABMD	46.44	2,929.67	(10,000.00)	9,431.52			(568.48)			-5.7%			
9/28/2018	ABMD	449.75	2,913.98	(10,000.00)	9,404.56			(595.44)			-6.0%			
9/28/2018	ALGN	391.22	2,913.98	(10,000.00)	9,380.14			(619.86)			-6.2%			
10/12/2018	ADBE	248.87	2,767.13	(10,000.00)	9,675.33			(324.67)			-3.2%			
10/12/2018	HQY	63.48	2,767.13	(10,000.00)	9,803.55			(196.45)			-2.0%			
10/12/2018	PANW	211.95	2,767.13	(10,000.00)	9,214.91			(785.09)			-7.9%			
10/12/2018	MDSO	37.85	2,767.13	(10,000.00)	9,407.70			(592.30)			-5.9%			
1/4/2019	TEAM	83.09	2,549.69	(20,000.00)	21,127.57			1,127.57			5.6%			
1/4/2019	CRM	137.96	2,549.69	(20,000.00)	23,298.06			3,298.06			16.5%			
1/4/2019	NOW	179.23	2,549.69	(20,000.00)	23,449.20			3,449.20			17.2%			
1/11/2019	INVA	19.30	2,596.26	(20,000.00)	18,877.71			(1,123.29)			-5.6%			
2/1/2019	CRM	155.87	2,706.32	(20,000.00)	20,621.08			621.08			3.1%			
2/1/2019	TEAM	98.98	2,706.32	(20,000.00)	22,495.45			2,495.45			12.5%			
2/1/2019	NOW	221.51	2,706.32	(20,000.00)	21,208.07			1,208.07			6.0%			
2/1/2019	PANW	220.27	2,706.32	(20,000.00)					2,214.55		11.1%			
2/1/2019	BEAT	72.34	2,706.32	(20,000.00)	20,583.26			583.26			2.9%			
2/1/2019	TTD	145.26	2,706.32	(20,000.00)	20,126.67			126.67			0.6%			
2/1/2019	FTNT	78.90	2,706.32	(20,000.00)	21,067.17			1,067.17			5.3%			
2/8/2019	PP	58.30	2,707.88	(20,000.00)	21,096.22			1,096.22			5.5%			
2/8/2019	VEEV	113.21	2,707.88	(20,000.00)	20,604.11			604.11			3.0%			
2/15/2019	ABMD	362.06	2,775.60	(20,000.00)	19,226.65			(773.35)			-3.9%			
2/15/2019	KL	33.59	2,775.60	(20,000.00)	21,000.30			1,000.30			5.0%			
2/15/2019	SSNC	59.76	2,775.60	(20,000.00)	19,263.56			(736.44)			-3.9%			
2/22/2019	ABMD	352.60	2,792.67	(20,000.00)	19,742.48			(257.52)			-1.3%			
2/22/2019	ANET	254.97	2,792.67	(20,000.00)	22,872.31			2,872.31			14.4%			
2/22/2019	HQY	60.29	2,792.67	(20,000.00)	20,718.99			718.99			3.6%			
2/22/2019	SSNC	59.83	2,792.67	(20,000.00)	19,185.04			(814.96)			-4.1%			
3/1/2019	NOW	243.52	2,803.69	(20,000.00)	23,304.90			304.90			1.2%			
3/22/2019	SSNC	62.14	2,800.71	(25,000.00)					1,267.30		5.1%			
3/22/2019	PAGS	29.59	2,800.71	(25,000.00)	24,594.45			(405.34)			-1.6%			
3/22/2019	AMZN	1,764.77	2,800.71	(25,000.00)	25,226.38			226.38			0.9%			
4/5/2019	ANET	311.06	2,892.24	(25,000.00)					1,101.88		4.4%			
4/5/2019	KLAC	124.34	2,892.24	(25,000.00)	24,817.03			(182.97)			-0.7%			

WORK CITED

(advfn.com) accumulation/distribution - page 1

(Investopedia.com) accumulation/distribution - page 1

(Investopedia.com) arms index – page 5

(Dinosaur technology and trading) average directional movement - page 9

(Stockcharts.com) average directional movement - page 9

(Stockcharts.com) Bollinger bands - page 13

(Investopedia.com) bulls vs. bears - page 17

Technical Analysis from A to Z: bulls vs. bears – page 17

(Chaikenpowertools.com) Chaiken money flow - page 19

(advfn.com) Commodity channel index - page.23

(Stockcharts.com) commodity channel index – page 23

(Investopedia.com) Fibonacci - page 31

(Investopedia.com) overview high low formula – page 35

(Investopedia.com) overview interpretation - page 35

(advfn.com) moving averages - page 39

(Vidiforex.com) forex trading analysis open 10 TRIN trading index – page 51

(Vidiforex.com) Market in and out open 10 TRIN - page 51

(ifcmarkets.com) Parabolic SAR - page 57

(Stockcharts.com) Parabolic SAR – page 57

(Stockcharts.com) pivot points - page 61

(advfn.com) price momentum - page 65

(Stockcharts.com) price momentum - page 65

(Investopedia.com) price momentum – page 65

(Stockcharts.com) pring's know sure thing - page 69

(Stockcharts.com) rate of change - page 73

(Wikipedia.org) relative strength index - page 77

(Wikipedia.org) stochastic oscillator - page 81

(Stockcharts.com) Time to trade true & strength formula – page 85

(Forexmentor.com) chart trend lines – page 85

(Investopedia.com) vix formula - page 91

(Investopedia.com) volume – page 93

(Investopedia.com) Pivot points - page 95

(Stock charts.com) Fibonacci – page 99

(cboe.com) Options – pages 109 to 121

(IBD.com) stock checkup composite rating – page 167

(IBD.com) stock checkup EPS rating - page 167

(IBD.com) stock checkup relative strength rating - page 167

(IBD.com) stock checkup SMR rating - page 168

(IBD.com) stock checkup accumulation/distribution rating – page 168

(IBD.com) checkup industry group rating - page 168

(IBD.com) stock checkup Estimate revision - page 168

(IBD.com) top 50 – page 171

(IBD.com) top 20 – page 171

(IBD.com) market direction group rs rating - page 178

(IBD.com) Number of quarters of EPS acceleration - page 178

(IBD.com) EPS estimate% change (current quarter) - page 178

(IBD.com) Estimated revision - page 178

(IBD.com) 3years EPS growth rate – page 178

(IBD.com) SMR rating – page 178

(IBD.com) Annual ROE - page 179

(IBD.com) Rs rating - page 179

(IBD.com) Supply and Demand – page 180

Legal Disclaimer

TERMS AND CONDITIONS Tech smart the perfect storm by John R Connelly and its members, officers, directors, owners, employees, agents, representatives, suppliers and service providers provide this for informational purposes only. Use of and access to this book and the information, materials, services, and other content available on or through the book or Site ("Content") are subject to these terms of use and all applicable laws.

NO INVESTMENT ADVICE The Content is for informational purposes only, you should not construe any such information or other material as legal, tax, investment, financial, or other advice. Nothing contained in this book or on our Site constitutes a solicitation, recommendation, endorsement, or offer by John R Connelly or any third party service provider to buy or sell any securities or other financial instruments in this or in any other jurisdiction in which such solicitation or offer would be unlawful under the securities laws of such jurisdiction. All Content on this book is information of a general nature and does not address the circumstances of any individual or entity. Nothing in the book constitutes professional and/or financial advice, nor does any information on the Site constitute a comprehensive or complete statement of the matters discussed or the law relating thereto. John R Connelly is not a fiduciary by virtue of any person's use of or access to the Site or Content in the book. You alone assume the sole responsibility of evaluating the merits and risks associated with the use of any information or other Content in the book or on the Site before making any decisions based on such information or other Content. Tech smart the perfect storm is provided for information purposes only it is not designed to provide any monetary value or gains; any investment should be made by a financial professional. When purchasing or reading the content in this book, you agree not to hold, John R Connelly, his affiliates or any third party service provider liable for any possible claim for damages arising from any decision you make based on information or other Content made available to you through the book.

INVESTMENT RISKS There are risks associated with investing in securities. Investing in stocks, bonds, exchange traded funds, mutual funds, and money market funds involve risk of loss. Loss of principal is possible. Some high-risk investments may use leverage, which will accentuate gains & losses. Foreign investing involves special risks, including a greater volatility and political, economic and currency risks and differences in accounting methods. John R Connelly's book tech smart the perfect storm, offers tools for making investment decision, however past investment performance is not a guarantee or predictor of future investment performance.

LIMITED RIGHT OF USE/OWNERSHIP OF CONTENT You are permitted to use the book and Content for your personal, non-commercial use only. The books information shall remain the property of John R Connelly and is protected by copyright, trademark, patent, and/or other intellectual property, proprietary, work product rights and laws. You may use the book and Content for your personal, noncommercial use, provided that you keep intact all copyright, trademark, patent and other proprietary notices.

CPSIA information can be obtained
at www.ICGtesting.com
Printed in the USA
LVHW112015200120
644177LV00005B/471